PIT STOP
AND OLIVE PITS

A literary license to enjoy driving
escapades throughout scenic Italy

JOHN TABELLIONE

GEMELLI PRESS

Published by Gemelli Press LLC
9600 Stone Avenue North
Seattle, Washington 98103

ISBN: 978-0-9864390-3-2
Library of Congress Control Number: pending

Cover Design by Partners in Design, Seattle, WA

PIT STOPS, PITFALLS AND OLIVE PITS

A literary license to enjoy driving escapades throughout scenic Italy

CONTENTS

L'INTRODUZIONE 9

PART I
A FRIENDLY SPIN AROUND ITALY

CHAPTER ONE. 14
Renting a Car & Getting on the Autostrada
(Rome)

CHAPTER TWO 20
High-Altitude Driving, Side-View Mirrors, & Family Reunions
(Pescara & Musellaro, Abruzzo)

CHAPTER THREE 28
Navigating the Amalfi Coast

CHAPTER FOUR 35
Stop Sign Protocol
(Pompeii)

CHAPTER FIVE. 38
Best. Italian. Meal. Ever.
(Calabria)

CHAPTER SIX 46
Taking Your Car on the Ferry
(Sicily)

CHAPTER SEVEN. 52
Eureka! A Family Reunion
(Siracusa, Sicily)

CHAPTER EIGHT 58
Maps, Signs, & Getting Directions
(Agrigento, Sicily)

CHAPTER NINE 64
Airport Reconnaissance
(Palermo, Sicily)

PART II
ANOTHER SPIN AROUND ITALY,
NOW WITH OFFSPRING!

CHAPTER TEN 70
Shifting Gears & One-Lane Road Right of Way
(Torgiano, Umbria)

CHAPTER ELEVEN 75
Family Reunion *Numero Tre*
(Musellaro, Abruzzo)

CHAPTER TWELVE 80
Toll Booth
(Arezzo, Tuscany)

CHAPTER THIRTEEN 85
Driving Under the Tuscan Sun
(Cortona, Tuscany)

CHAPTER FOURTEEN 90
Parking & Street Racing
(Montecatini Terme, Tuscany)

CHAPTER FIFTEEN 95
Knowing When to Park & Walk
(Lucca & San Gimignano, Tuscany)

CHAPTER SIXTEEN 102
Horse(power) of a Different Color
(Siena, Tuscany)

CHAPTER SEVENTEEN 107
Checking the Brakes
(Le Cinque Terre)

CHAPTER EIGHTEEN 113
Buying Self-Serve Fuel on Sundays & Returning the Rental Car
 (Bologna)

HOTEL GUIDE 117
ACKNOWLEDGMENTS 123
PHOTO CREDITS 124
GLOSSARY 125
AUTHOR BIOGRAPHY 128

VENEZIA

BOLOGNA
LUCCA
MONTECATINI
FIRENZE

MILANO
LE CINQUE TERRE
PISA
SAN GIMIGNANO
SIENA

CORTONA
PERUGIA

Italy

TORGIANO

PESCARA
MUSELLARO

ROMA

NAPOLI
POMPEII
RAVELLO

MESSINA
PALERMO

MARTONE
MARINA DI GIOIOSA IONICA
REGGIO DI CALABRIA
TAORMINA

AGRIGENTO
SIRACUSA

L'INTRODUZIONE

If there is a specific scene that captures the essence and serendipity of driving in Italy, it just may be this one that occurred in Naples, featuring a Sophia Loren look-alike.

Dressed in a stylish, short skirt, a sleeveless, white blouse and wearing stiletto heels, our beauty is spotted driving her sporty Vespa at a busy city intersection. She notices her (presumed) boyfriend's car at a red light and comes to a complete stop behind him. Then she jumps off her scooter and runs up to him.

They embrace, kiss, and talk intimately for several minutes.

Meanwhile, several Neapolitan commuters, now stuck in line, are getting an eyeful, but then quickly grow irritated. Horns start blaring; a few shouts emerge from their open windows. A few more moments pass before the couple finally kisses good-bye longingly.

Realizing her impatient audience is practically on the verge of spitting, she proceeds to do what comes naturally to her: before she hops aboard her Vespa she showers several two-handed, animated kisses to all of the motorists and cyclists as a gesture of thanks for their time.

The drivers astride their scooters and in their cars immediately change their attitudes and respond, most appropriately, with a round of applause in appreciation—this time with lighter, positive toots of their horns.

What this story tells us is to expect the unexpected from those passionate Italian drivers, whether in the city, along the Amalfi Coast, or in *il centro* (the center) of a medieval village.

I know this to be true because I have had the wonderful experience of driving throughout Italy from Bologna to Basilicata, Le Cinque Terre to Calabria, and from Tuscany to Taormina, Sicily. And to several other places in between that are not on the map (at least I couldn't find them on mine).

My purpose in writing this roadside/bedside travel handbook is to encourage you to try driving in Italy yourself and enjoy the history and scenery as you can only do by automobile. When you're on a cruise, you have to be back in time before the ship's departure. The same goes for bus tours and train schedules.

Should you choose to drive, however, you own *la strada, the road.* You can stop at any tiny hill town that captures your imagination and then linger at your leisure. Or you might look up those long-lost relatives and savor outdoor dining late into the evening, the way Italians know best.

Within this guidebook is a collection of personal anecdotes that knit together place and purpose with a summary paragraph at the end of each chapter, which I term a "Pit Tip" to help with your road trip. The stories focus on my travel adventures with family and dear friends throughout Italy. As you ride along with us in the book, we will take two motor trips: one with our friends Joe and Jean and the other with our adult son, Jay. (No, your name doesn't have to begin with "J" to be able to travel in Italy.) We will travel north to south through several locales, events, and subjects in order to illustrate the rules of the road.

Along the way we'll meet some larger than life people: Vinnie, a fellow veterinarian of our friend, Joe; cousins Little Tommy; Gino and his wife, Filomena; Adolfo and his wife, Mariella; their families; and an expatriate friend, Chris. Throw in a friendly toll booth manager, an octogenarian Sicilian cart driver, a couple of *carabinieri* (Italian military police officers) and you have a cast of characters to fall in love with. You will get to meet some of our Italian relatives and learn how wonderful family reunions can be as they share their homes and delicious food (if you're also lucky enough to be of Italian descent).

Travel with us the length of Italy down to and all around Sicily, plus several interesting points in between these sites. You will pick up a few key vocabulary words to help you start your basic Italian lessons.

My wish is that by sharing these humorous, serendipitous experiences, I might inspire you to want to emulate them—except, of course, for the mistakes and getting lost. Then again, losing your way is not totally bad, as you will soon realize with all your senses.

Above all, my best advice is to drive safely and defensively and have a lot of fun disproving the fallacy that all roads lead to Rome.

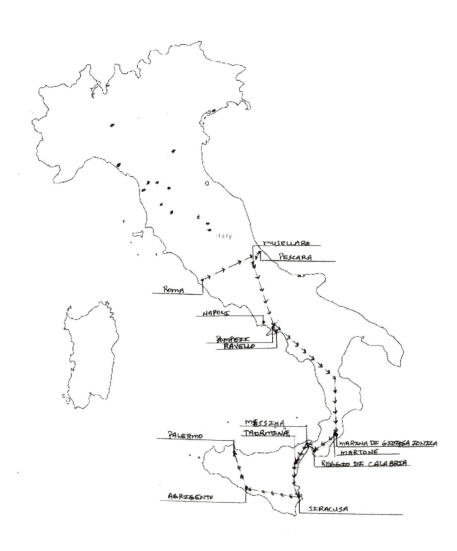

PART I

A FRIENDLY SPIN AROUND ITALY

CHAPTER ONE

Renting a Car & Getting on the Autostrada

(Rome)

Even though my wife, Jackie, had made all the arrangements before leaving home, renting a car in Rome became no small matter for us. First, Jackie and I, along with our traveling companions, Jean and Joe, had to reconnoiter our way through the halls of *Roma Termini, Rome's sprawling train station,* passing underneath the tracks through a tunnel and then walking the entire length of the station on the other side to look for the rental car office, which ended up being run by . . . Signor Randazzo?

I couldn't help laughing to myself when I saw his name plate. In the obscure but hilarious Roberto Benigni comedy, *Johnny Stecchino,* Randazzo was the name of the fictitious insurance bureaucrat who harassed Johnny about his bogus worker's compensation claim. Randazzo's real-life namesake lived up to his reputation and gave us a major league, bureaucratic runaround about insurance, forms, waivers, and pricing before we finally got the rental contract settled and signed.

At last, we started to load the trunk of our shiny, cherry-red Alfa Romeo. Jean and Joe's two smaller suitcases and our one large suitcase fit snugly in the trunk, and somehow, as the trip progressed, we even managed to squeeze gifts, souvenirs, and *limoncello* (lemon liqueur) bottles into this cramped storage area.

As we began to get into the car, however, we barely avoided being red-faced again with Signor Randazzo. Noticing a distinct lack of back doors, Jackie and Jean concluded that Randazzo had indeed swindled the four unsuspecting American tourists by renting us a two-door coupe instead of the sedan we had reserved.

Just as they began to march back into the rental car office to give Randazzo yet another piece of their collective minds, Joe and I saved them from making a bad impression or, as it is better captured in Italian, *brutta figura*. We discovered that the Italian designers had indeed included another pair of doors, but they featured handles stylishly recessed behind the rear windows, toward the trunk end of the car. We had all been looking for the exposed handles in their customary American car locations.

Apparently the Italians design their vehicles with style inserted in every detail, right down to the door openers. Little did we know.

And so we buckled up, ready for the challenges of our Roman road rally. Now the question was: were we ready for the modern day version of the chariot races? Instead of having a chase at the site of the ruins of the Circus Maximus, however, it was on an even more treacherous venue: a main concourse with six lanes of traffic racing in the same direction. Italians may well be the warmest, most loving people on Earth, but they change personalities, often for the worse, when they get behind the wheel.

As if the sheer volume of traffic was not nerve-racking enough, no one was staying within the space of their lanes. Still, with Joe driving and three passenger sets of eyes to spot road signs, in less than a very tense quarter of an hour we miraculously succeeded in finding our hotel. After our short initiation in the Grand Prix of Rome, we decided to rest before tackling Rome's sights on foot or let the city's taxi drivers do their things.

•

The next morning we set out early for a trek on Rome's cobblestone back streets, to peek into alleyways, and to follow our exploring instincts: an outdoor café tucked into an intimate corner of two buildings with a few patrons sipping cappuccino; an antique store with a window display of medieval armor; and enchanting private villas with wrought iron gates through which we stare in awe like kids in a candy store.

All during this time our chatter was an alternating mix of history and the present, the here and now of the four of us, exploring the wonders of ancient Rome, then a memory of our children growing up, good times together, then back to the Fall of Rome. No, not the decline of the Roman Empire; rather, Jean slipping on the uneven, cobblestone street surface and taking an embarrassing spill.

Fortunately, she suffered no injuries, and we proceeded geographically and chronologically to the Pantheon, Piazza Navona, and the popular Trevi Fountain into which we throw coins over our left shoulders, like all good tourists, to guarantee a return visit. Lastly we made a stop at a modern day treat late in the afternoon: the best gelato in all of Rome, located right around the corner from Trevi.

We reserved the following day for the Vatican. The Sistine Chapel received its name from Pope Sixtus IV who had it restored between 1477 and 1480. About thirty years later, Michelangelo painted the now-famous ceiling under the patronage of Pope Julius II. Ironically, Michelangelo didn't consider himself much of a painter, except perhaps once in a competition in Florence against Leonardo da Vinci. (No winner was declared because a war had broken out before Michelangelo could finish.)

So when the Pope commissioned him to paint the ceiling of the Chapel, he did so somewhat begrudgingly. If there had been bumper stickers in his era, Michelangelo's might have read: "I'd rather be sculpting."

For centuries, forces of nature worked to decay the art of the Sistine Chapel until it was restored to its original colors during the 1980s and 1990s. However, certain areas of the ceiling remained unrestored, illustrating the "before and after"—truly like night and day. To better preserve the Chapel's artwork, St. Peter's officials forbid photography and appeal for reverence and silence while tourists are viewing it.

Michelangelo also left his mark inside the Basilica with his Carrara marble sculpture, *Pietà*, which he completed as a young man, decades before he got involved with construction of the mother church of Roman Catholicism. We were fortunate to see St. Peter's without the crowds for Mass and were still awestruck by the Vatican the following day when it was time to say *"Arrivederci, Roma!"*

I mention all the details of St. Peter's beauty to explain why we had such trouble that evening wrapping our heads around the sheer chaos that was the streets of Rome—our previous small taste of the Grand Prix was nothing compared to what we were about to face after a late check-out from our hotel.

Again with Joe at the wheel, we somehow managed to pass unscathed through a few harrowing intersections in the Eternal City without missing our turns. When he turned onto a main concourse, we entered the now-familiar six loosely defined lanes of vehicles.

We maneuvered through a mess that resembled a wide open field of cars at a race track barreling at a hundred kilometers an hour. Romans, we confirmed, are not good lane drivers. After a stressful, horn-honking-filled half hour, Joe miraculously succeeded in merging onto the *autostrada*, the highway, heading due east towards the Adriatic and the region of Abruzzo—home to my ancestors and present-day relatives.

Pit Tip: Always make your rental car reservation before your trip and don't leave home without it. There is a fee for a second driver of a rental car, so plan for that as well.

Before pulling out of the rental place, always check the car and make sure you understand where all of the controls are and what they do.

The option of a navigational system can be helpful, but might add 25-30% to the rental. Also, sometimes, a GPS may actually run slower than your actual speed, causing you to go past a turn. Furthermore, having a GPS can take away from the spontaneity and adventure of possibly getting lost in a tiny, quaint village off the beaten track.

And finally, as part of your pre-trip planning, don't forget that Italy requires drivers who don't have an EU driver's license to carry one from their home country as well as an International Driver's Permit, easily obtainable from AAA or the National Automobile Club for a small fee.

Pit Tip: When driving in Rome, be prepared to encounter something similar to the chariot races once held at the Circus Maximus. Their descendants, friendly and personable as a whole, go through a metamorphosis and take on a daredevil personality when behind the wheel.

In fact, if you can avoid driving in Rome at all, do so. The only time you ever want to drive in Rome is to get out of town. Otherwise, take public transportation or walk. Rome is truly a walkable city with wonderful surprises around every corner.

CHAPTER TWO

High-Altitude Driving, Side-View Mirrors, & Family Reunions

(Pescara & Musellaro, Abruzzo)

The ride on the autostrada from Rome to the Abruzzo Region on the Adriatic Sea started peacefully enough. We felt as if we were on a highway to heaven, discovering fascinating, scenic vistas of hilltop castles, churches, and villages built in medieval times. Then we began to ascend through the majestic Apennines, and as we did, we prayed that the Italian engineers who designed and built the highway graduated *col massimi dei voti* (highest honors) from college.

How can I best describe the mile-high (or so it seemed) concrete trestle bridges that supported the highway system? As the road curved ahead of us, we could see what laid beneath us, or better still, what was not under us: just thin air. The ribbon of highway stretched ahead of us for kilometers at a time, occasionally entering and exiting through tunnel after tunnel, as if nothing supported the links of the concrete and steel highway except, thankfully, gigantic viaducts every few hundred meters.

I felt proud of not only the Italian engineers as we sped towards our destination, but also for the beautiful terrain of my ancestral land. The wonders of the countryside, including the Abruzzo National Park, surrounded us through most of the two-and-a-half-hour drive and left our jaws hanging open many times over.

Mountain peaks of over six-thousand feet rose majestically over the landscape filled with forests, streams and lakes. Covering five-hundred square kilometers, the Parco Nazionale d'Abruzzo is one of Italy's largest national parks and offers a variety of outdoor activities, including skiing, hiking, horseback riding, and canoeing. Animal life includes bears, wolves, and wild boar. Fortunately, we didn't encounter any of these Italian natives.

Over a hundred years ago, my grandparents covered these overland routes in rudimentary, horse-and-cart transportation to reach Naples in order to set sail for America. Now, as their American offspring, I found myself returning to drive through this picturesque land to search for roots, looking forward to meeting my Italian cousins.

I wondered whether they were as much in awe of the natural beauty that surrounded them as I was.

•

Pulling off the highway into the city of Pescara on the Adriatic gave me a double pleasure. First, I was setting foot in the area of Italy where my grandparents were born, and second, I was excited to see and experience this vibrant city with its split personality. Pescara consists of three diverse areas: a modern seacoast resort complete with Prada-class boutiques; a university town; and a successful industrialized area.

One major drawback, however, came with the introduction of another form of Italian driving mania: narrow streets with cars parked on both sides, often with the right set of tires sitting on the curb. Joe was at the wheel, painstakingly driving at a crawl pace as he negotiated our Alfa Romeo through such a neighborhood street, which was the scene of an accident just prior to our arrival.

To add more flavor, all the drivers were simultaneously honking their horns, venting at the mishap and at a delivery truck that was double-parked. We thought we were doing well until we heard a moaning, groaning, crunching sound of metal against metal—on our car. Fortunately, it was just a slowly approaching car's rearview mirror bumping ours and folding it back on its hinge.

We successfully found our hotel and had the immediate pleasure of meeting Bruno, the manager of the Plaza, who spoke perfect English and exuded sincere Italian charm. Procter and Gamble has a plant in Pescara, and American business people frequently stayed at this hotel, so Bruno knew English almost as well as his native tongue.

He gave us a very warm welcome as we introduced ourselves and explained our reason for stopping in Pescara. In fact, he even offered to call a couple of phone numbers my Uncle Jerry, who had visited here a couple of times, had given me.

After a hearty breakfast in the hotel restaurant the next morning, we found Bruno still manning the front desk. We didn't know what to expect with the phone calls since we hadn't notified anyone in advance, didn't know exactly how far Pescara was from their homes, or how much time our schedule might allow. Not to mention that none of us spoke Italian fluently.

The first number we gave him connected to two elderly ladies in the countryside. They were very skeptical that some distant American relatives had mysteriously arrived in Pescara, unannounced, just to say hello. They weren't buying that story, nor did they trust that someone from a hotel in the big city was calling. It all sounded too much like the beginnings of a scam to them so that was that.

Next, Bruno telephoned Gino Tabellione, my seventy-seven-year-old cousin, who lived closer to the hotel and, fortunately, he believed him. Gino promised to come in an hour. We couldn't believe our luck.

Sure enough, less than an hour later, Gino, the former postmaster of Rosciano, a nearby suburb, showed up dressed in a suit, but without a tie, and accompanied by his adult daughter Claudia. He looked a lot like my late Uncle Nick and also a little like my cousin Joseph.

We found ourselves holding a family reunion hosted by Bruno in the lobby of the Plaza Hotel. We showed pictures of my Uncle Jerry and Aunt Lucy who had visited Gino several years prior. Then I started to draw family trees to make all of the connections between my father and his brothers and sisters. Gino's father, Bernardino, and my father's father, Giustino, were brothers. Several times Gino mentioned that we should say "hi" to my uncle, and I promised we would.

After a while, he invited us to his house, so Claudia drove Jackie and Jean while Gino came with Joe and me in our car. After he retired, he moved to the city of Pescara. His lovely wife, Filomena, offered us espresso when we reached their very nice apartment overlooking the Adriatic. One of their five children, Marco, was a professor at the University of Pescara, and Gino proudly showed us one of Marco's published books of poems.

It took a titanic effort to converse without Bruno available to translate, but somehow we managed with pictures, family trees, dictionaries, and charades. For instance, I spent ten minutes describing my occupation involving walls, doors, and windows by pointing at them. They took this to mean I was a carpenter, but I was really trying to explain that I worked for a building products company. Finally, when I motioned as if I were writing on paper, Gino correctly interpreted my hand signals that I was *rappresentante*, a salesman.

After we finished our espresso, they insisted we stay for lunch and more. I politely explained, though, relatively easily in my broken Italian, the arrival time and the next destination on our journey: the Amalfi Coast, which remained several hours away. So we said our good-byes and headed back toward the autostrada.

•

But remember those two sisters who had been suspicious of American relatives coming to visit? We couldn't resist trying to catch up with them in their tiny hamlet of Musellaro, so within an hour it was time to "Meet the Grandparents"—or at least the birthplace of my grandparents.

My Uncle Jerry had mentioned that the hometown of my grandma and grandpa had a castle and a church high on a hill (like so many other towns). As we approached that area and spotted such a castle and church high above us, we decided to get off the autostrada and explore the vicinity, which we learned was where my cousin Gino's two sisters live. The gorgeous zigzag route took us up the mountain past vineyards and grazing sheep until we finally arrived at the picturesque village of Bolognano, situated halfway up the mountain, well below Musellaro.

We continued our climb and stopped at the outskirts of town to take a picture standing next to the Musellaro road sign. A young guy, who turned out to be a college student in Pescara and who spoke a little English, greeted us outside of his home where we had stopped. With our minimal Italian, we explained we were looking for the Tabellione residence. Since Musellaro is merely a burg with a couple hundred houses and people, he knew everyone, and he pointed down the road to the family house. We thanked him for his time and assistance.

Apparently, Gino had called his sisters to let them know we were in town, so they were not totally shocked when we arrived at their homes. In fact, Laurina and Santina welcomed us rather warmly. We were not able to determine if Laurina was a widow or never married, but we learned that Santina was wedded to Emilio, and the two siblings lived in adjacent houses. All three were in their seventies but spry with warm personalities. Their frequent smiles melted the language barrier.

They insisted we visit the town's church, the site of my grandparents' wedding, a kilometer down the road; Laurina was the caretaker, so she led the way. Even though I helped her climb the long series of steps leading to the church by holding her arm, she was really nimble enough to make it on her own. She did this same trek every day of her life, after all.

A beautiful chapel with wonderful paintings and stained glass windows that tell a local religious story, this church had been part of a nobleman's castle when he donated it several hundred years ago.

Tradition had it that it was the site of a miraculous Bleeding Crucifix that dated back to the Crusades.

They wanted us to stay longer, but we had to leave. We took several pictures to capture these wonderful people—part of our family—for our memories. In a sense, it really was not necessary. To this day, I can still see in my mind's eye these lovable relatives (plus Gino and his family). I can also vividly recall the sight of their vineyards, their modest stucco dwellings, that special chapel in the castle and the beautiful mountainsides, which rival the scenery in *The Sound of Music*.

We finally took off for the Amalfi Coast by late afternoon, heading back toward Rome on the *autostrada*, and then toward Naples. The bucolic scenery, the mountains, the tunnels and the extremely high bridges made for a dramatic ride as we recapped our unlikely family reunions.

Pit Tip: If you find yourself driving through the Parco Nazionale d'Abruzzo, and I highly recommend you do, don't look down. Keep looking straight ahead as the ribbon of highway stretches for kilometers, entering and exiting a series of tunnels. Moreover, when driving through tunnels, respect speed limits and keep a safe distance from other vehicles. Be aware that tunnels have emergency exits and SOS Points.

Pit Tip: **If you happen to be looking up long-lost relatives, give them a heads up so they can better prepare for your visit.** Make the effort to climb every mountain, ford every stream to meet them or trace your ancestry. You'll be so glad you did. Don't let language be a roadblock to having a great time, but seriously consider taking a course in Italian before you leave home for at least the basics.

Pit Tip: So you think you can speak the language of Dante better than a fifth grader? Asking a basic question for directions, such as where to find something, "***Dov'è*** . . . (fill in the word)?" is the easy part. Being prepared for an onslaught of rapid Italian in response is another. If you do not speak the language very well, don't be afraid to use your hands; Italians do so quite a bit, even when conversing in their native tongue to each other.

CHAPTER THREE

Navigating the Amalfi Coast

Fresh off our family reunion with Gino and his family, Jackie, Jean, Joe, and I anxiously approached the Amalfi Coast and its legendary narrow, ever-winding road carved into sheer cliffs. We were rewarded with a breathtaking view of the sun setting on the azure Tyrrhenian Sea. A series of promontories blanketed with clusters of lemon groves wherever villagers could find the slightest patch of soil jut out of the water to sharply define the coastline.

Meanwhile, we encountered another shocking Italian driving experience. We had to ever-so-carefully downshift into second gear to about twenty to twenty-five miles per hour to maneuver along the twisty road carved into mountainside. Even at that slow rate, we came to an abrupt stop at a hairpin turn where a huge tour bus emerged from a hidden curve and headed directly toward us.

Another such switchback and head-on bus confrontation occurred a few miles ahead within a small tunnel. Our only warning was a blast of the approaching vehicle's horn combined with a distorted shape of a windshield and headlights reflected in a huge, angled mirror mounted above the exit mouth of the mini-cave.

We continued our crawl for a few uneventful minutes until our nerves again took a jolt. A "suicidal" Vespa driver tried to overtake us, practically daring us to race him along one "Dead Man's Curve" after another. We let him win.

Heading west, then north along the coast, we instinctively hugged the hillside while those headed in the opposite direction have a safety guard rail: a mere three-foot high curbing. For good measure, a few pedestrians on their evening strolls added to the mix, and there we were: a carload of four American tourists with their hearts in their stomachs.

We managed to safely arrive in Maiori where we had reservations at the Casa Raffaele Conforti. This villa, built in the nineteenth century, originally served as home to a rich lemon merchant. The décor of the rooms featured antique furnishings of the original Conforti family, which still owns and manages the property. The bed chambers had fifteen-foot high ceilings and walls lavishly decorated with Baroque-era frescoes. Double doors nearly as high and festooned with wind-blown sheers opened to our respective balconies. Antique Venetian glass chandeliers that acted as prisms catching the fading rays of the day's sun provided lighting for these romantic rooms. Such lavish quarters gave us a sense of royalty we never expected given the reasonable room rate.

As we relaxed over a glass of wine on our adjoining wrought iron balconies adorned with seasonal flower pots, we faced a bit of down-to-earth reality. We started to ponder the next day's dilemma. We were planning to drive up the coastline to the classical town of Ravello, but we had booked the Conforti for two consecutive nights. That itinerary meant we would have to return southward along the coast with the sheer cliffs immediately to our right. Still in shock from our hair-raising arrival experience, we couldn't comprehend driving on the cliff side of the road. We tried our hardest to get out of our second night's stay, but the hotel's owners weren't going for it without charging us.

Realizing we had no alternative but to do the round-trip along the coast the next day, Joe exclaimed quite succinctly, "We're dead in the water," to which I immediately retorted: "Joe! Please don't use that expression here around the Amalfi Coast." The nervous laughter that followed broke the tension and allowed us to enjoy a delicious, traditional *pizza margherita* with tomato sauce, mozzarella, and basil for dinner, followed by our introductory taste of the deliciously addictive lemon liqueur, *limoncello.*

As it turned out, we had nothing to fear since Joe took to the Amalfi Coast like Mario Andretti, and we zigged and zagged our way with everyone's right foot acting as an extra brake—just in case. Maiori is situated right at sea level, and as we departed, the road immediately began climbing higher and higher.

After about twenty kilometers, we came upon the exit for Ravello. From there, we took a tertiary country road on an even more tortuous winding ascent up the mountainside, gasping in awe. The breathtaking beauty, the scent of the lemon trees, and the coastline fell away farther from our vantage point. I got the sensation as in a dream that our car could almost tip backwards if we were all to turn and look out the rear window at once. Eventually, we arrived at a parking area on level ground and begin to traverse as the locals wisely do: on foot.

A classic piazza in front of a church served as our welcoming site with pedestrian walkways beckoning us in all directions to shops, gardens, castles, and more. The secret of Ravello's enticing beauty has been known to Europeans for centuries. Wagner composed his *Parsifal* there, leading to a tradition of holding an annual music fest in his honor. D.H. Lawrence vacationed in Ravello, seeking inspiration.

Now we had discovered it as a cultural awakening for ourselves as part of our Grand Tour. Even as we shopped, we learned about the history of the town, as well as about the arts of *majolica* pottery and fine paper-making known throughout the Amalfi region. We followed one path to the Villa Cimbrone, a magnificent castle-turned-hotel with gardens and vistas that left the rest of us as speechless as Jean, who was suffering from oncoming laryngitis.

At one end of the gardens, we approached the *Terrace of Infinity*: a waist-high, marble wall on which a series of busts of people of Italian notoriety are positioned every fifty feet or so and which provides a view that American writer Gore Vidal has called "the most beautiful view in the world." As we cautiously approached the wall and turned our backs to the sea to pose for a photo, we got a sinking feeling that we were on the edge of a sheer drop-off, and we each took a deep breath to overcome our emotional high.

For lunch, we discovered a restaurant nestled on the mountainside where we dined outside. We delighted in *gnocchi (potato dumplings)* stuffed with ricotta cheese. Simultaneously, our other senses kicked in and we began to appreciate the proximity of gorgeous, exotic, perfumed flowers and wind-shaped trees, while in the distant haze we viewed the Tyrrhenian Sea and neighboring villages far below us as if in a still-life painting. The scene was so entrancing we didn't want to leave even when we finished our meal, so we decided to sit spellbound a while longer, savoring the moment of a lifetime.

Returning to the main piazza, Jackie and Jean paused every few feet in the *giardini* (gardens) to comment on the beauty and intoxicating scents of the *fiori (flowers)*. Meanwhile, what came marching toward us through the central plaza, but the local oompah-pah band from Maiori, entertaining the tourists with a mix of classical and traditional Italian songs.

The music seemed to put everyone in a cheerful mood, so while Joe and I struck up a conversation with a local tobacconist named Andrea, Jackie and Jean took off to the shops to buy dishes made by artisans from Vietri, a village down the coast renowned for its ceramics. Thanks to a couple ladies they met from New Jersey, whom we discovered actually knew Jackie's cousin from their hometown of Westfield, Jackie and Jean accepted their word that the *bottega* (shop) they were in at the moment was the best place for prices and selection. These New Jerseyans had been to several towns and stores earlier to do comparison shopping. The shop-owner carefully wrapped our yellow-and-blue floral flat-dish purchases, which packed more easily into the trunk than large, round pasta bowls would have.

As evening shadows crept in, we felt sad to leave, not only to have to say *"ciao"* to Ravello's beauty, but also because we now had to head south, along the cragged coastline. As we meandered ever so slowly downhill, we all kept our feet on our collective brakes, almost afraid to talk. When we did speak, it was to say, "Careful!" or "Watch out!" Or, as Joe so articulately stated as we rounded a curve, heading into a tunnel, "We're between a rock and a hard spot!"

We returned safely to our palatial villa just before nightfall and decided to eat at the same *trattoria* (small restaurant) as the prior evening. This time we enjoyed delicious *farfalle* (butterfly) pasta topped with a savory egg and butter sauce. Our waiter once again supplied free *limoncello* after the meal, which prompted us to go shopping for a bottle or two for ourselves to take home.

We met one liquor merchant who spoke English with what we correctly detected to be a German accent. His mother had moved to this area of Campania from Germany. The four of us also shopped in another store where we had the chance to taste-test some of the other spirits. In doing so, we decided to add a unique fennel-based liqueur to our selection. We found the perfect spot for our four-pack of bottles: they fit snugly in a corner of the trunk over the wheel well.

The following morning we departed Casa Conforti after bidding farewell to, and tipping, our young, eager-to-please innkeepers, Francesco and Antoinetta.

Pit Tip: You don't need a BMW to motor along the Amalfi Coast. You'll still get the most unforgettable ultimate driving experience of a lifetime in a Fiat or an Alfa Romeo. Drive very carefully and savor every minute, every site, every bite, and every height along the Amalfi Coast. It's a breathtaking, thrilling ride you'll never forget.

Be sure to keep an eye out for "suicidal" Vespa drivers daring to race you along the ever-curvy road, all bordered by a mere three-foot high curbing—the only defense that stands between you and the Tyrrhenian Sea hundreds of feet below.

Once you're in the villages along the Amalfi Coast, your best bet is to make like the locals and walk. Should you ever have an accident or require immediate medical assistance, go to the ***pronto soccorso*** (emergency room) at the nearest ***ospedale*** **(hospital)**. For lesser maladies, you can get medical advice and medications from a local pharmacy (***farmacia),*** marked by a large, green cross (***croce verde***).

CHAPTER FOUR

Stop Sign Protocol

(Pompeii)

After two days of exploring the treasures of the Amalfi Coast, we exited the renowned, twisted, spaghetti-shaped road at Salerno and headed north on an inland route for a few miles. We approached the outskirts of Naples in order to reach Pompeii, the ancient city buried intact under the ash from Mt. Vesuvius nearly two thousand years ago. Pompeii's civilization may have been destroyed in a matter of a day by the cataclysmic eruption, yet the very fact that Vesuvius buried the town completely gives us an insightful glimpse of an advanced culture from several centuries ago.

First discovered in the late sixteenth century by Domenico Fontana, the Italian architect who designed the Vatican library, Pompeii has been the subject of several excavations that have unraveled its mystery. The people were not necessarily burned by lava and hot ashes; many were overcome by the noxious fumes of the volcano. Accordingly, Pompeii's citizens were preserved in place, many engaged in everyday tasks as demonstrated by casts made of several of the bodies.

Many of their structures have also been excavated. From all of these clues, we know of the advanced degree of society created by the Pompeiians. Not only did they have a prosperous economy, they also had a lifestyle comparable to today's standards with modern homes, running water, gardens, wall murals, pets, and religious rites (albeit mostly pagan).

During our visit, it was as if Joe was speaking through a layer of ash himself as he asked the guide at the information desk how the plumbing systems worked in the city before Vesuvius erupted. After being told that the men's room was located in the modern-day restaurant and gift shop, he raised his voice in broken Italian in the hopes of being better understood. The more Joe insisted he already knew the location of the bathrooms, the louder the guard spoke and more dramatically pointed to the back of the restaurant.

In the end, the answers to Joe's questions were found in the Pompeii guidebook he purchased, but he'll certainly never forget where the bathrooms are.

We returned to the parking lot where we had left our vehicle in the care of a guy who roamed around to keep an eye on people's cars. When we first parked, I was really leery but you get used to it. Miraculously, we found our trusty Alfa Romeo safe and sound.

However, a few minutes later, we survived our own near-calamity trying to drive out of this area of metropolitan Naples. At a four-way intersection, the traffic somehow ran safely and self-orchestrated, despite everyone ignoring their respective stop signs as if they didn't exist. Extricating our car from this skittish cha-cha presented a driving challenge to say the least.

Fortunately, with a little luck and a lot of patience, we progressed through that tangle of confusion and spotted the nearby *autostrada* heading south, where we proceeded to accelerate more to the tempo of a tarantella.

Pit Tip: When you come into a four-way intersection, if you see everyone else not stopping, keep moving as safely and cautiously as possible without hesitation. Of course, if there are police officers directing traffic, the best advice would be to heed their signals to avoid getting ***una multa*** (a ticket).

CHAPTER FIVE

Best. Italian. Meal. Ever.

(Calabria)

Destination: The tiny seacoast town of Marina di Gioiosa Ionica in Calabria, the hometown of Vinnie, Joe's friend and fellow veterinarian. It was my turn at the wheel that afternoon after a fascinating but tiring tour of Pompeii, and before I could say *"pasta e fagioli"* (pasta and beans), all my passengers were fast asleep.

Time after time I was tempted to awaken them as I drove high above lush valleys and through dozens of dark tunnels. Often the neighboring mountain peaks seemed to rise up within what seemed to be a stone's throw away from us. Upon spotting pinnacle after pinnacle upon pinnacle, I realized that the only way they could have designed this *autostrada* was through the mountain range. A highway on the valley floors would take drivers days to navigate around the bases of so many mountains.

So when in Rome, or on this day as we left Naples, don't do as they do on these freeways. That is, take off at high speeds as if you are flying instead of driving. I kept it at about 120 kilometers per hour and wisely moved to the right lane whenever a Mercedes or BMW with lights flashing came zooming up behind our Alfa Romeo.

By mid-afternoon it was time for a pit stop in the region of Basilicata, and we had the opportunity to exchange greetings and smiles with several priests and nuns at the rest area. Unfortunately for Jean, she did not have any small change to give to a cantankerous attendant at the wash station, which earned her a very nasty look when she tried to explain her situation. Luckily, she made change with us and tipped the lady a few moments later, or else we were all going to be on the wrong side of a primeval curse from the old crone.

After a couple more hours, around dusk, we exited the autostrada and crossed over a range of mountains toward the Ionian Sea. We found Gioiosa and the hotel Vinnie had recommended, which appeared practically deserted for the off-season. A major renovation was underway. The latest architectural marble and glass materials and an open staircase centered in the three-story atrium were prominent new additions.

While Joe and I checked into the hotel with our passports and forms, Jackie and Jean set out in desperate search of a bathroom. With suitcases rolling in tow, they tried to squeeze into an elevator the size of a linen closet. However, with no light inside, they immediately grew claustrophobic and silly and refused to close the elevator door.

Eventually, they realized that a light would turn on and the elevator would go up when they pressed a certain button. A few seconds later from the second floor, Jackie yelled down the stairwell, "The room has no bed, the light switch is not working, and oh by the way, Jean is barely holding on."

In my best Italian, I implored the hotel manager, *"In camera . . . no mattress-o!"*

He growled back, *"Impossibile!"* Impossible.

Jackie, of course, could hear him and again insisted, between giggles, that there was no bed from what she could or could not see because she only had the hallway lighting shining partway into the room.

He, in turn, repeated, *"Impossibile!"* and immediately dashed into the elevator to go up and prove his point. And prove it he did. A guest flipping a light switch doesn't necessarily mean "Let there be light," apparently.

He tromped over to a far wall in the darkened entranceway and inserted the plastic card he had given Jackie. Then, and only then, did the electricity flow.

Laughter, tears of silliness, and other elements also flowed for Jean.

Furthermore, now that the room was lit, Jackie realized that we indeed did have a complete suite. She had been squinting into the hallway, which is why it had appeared that there was no bed. The bedroom was to the side of that hallway.

•

After settling in, we got in touch with Joe's friend, Vinnie, and soon he was at our hotel to meet us with his girlfriend in her tiny, old Fiat as his car was in the shop. Vinnie, tanned and sporting a Boston Red Sox cap and a warm smile on his slightly bearded face, welcomed us and introduced everyone.

Vinnie had been born in Italy and educated at the University of Bologna but had gone to high school in the United States. He readily admitted that he spoke Italian with an American accent and English with an Italian accent. When Jean complimented the beauty of Vinnie's girlfriend, he explained that when he was in his twenties and thirties, he dated twenty-somethings. Now in his late forties, he still dated girls in their twenties, and, thus, we got an inkling of Vinnie's laid-back philosophy.

Cutting to the chase, Vinnie asked if we were hungry and upon seeing our eager faces, promised us a meal as good as his mother's cooking. His mom lived in Connecticut, though, so we had no idea how good her cooking might be. We just had to take our chances. We were starving.

We followed him up and around a small mountain, which lacked streetlights and had no side barrier. Finally, after several minutes of ascending, with the seaside town of Marina di Gioiosa Ionica twinkling several hundred meters below us, we reached a plateau upon which rested the even smaller hamlet of Martone.

We parked and followed Vinnie into a building that served as the town *trattoria* even though we could see no sign posted or painted outside. Why waste paint, explained Vinnie: Everyone in the town already knew what was inside La Collinetta, which means "little hill."

In Martone, the locals rarely see Americans so we became the center of attention as we gathered at a table. Handsome farmers, merchants, young families with infants—they all warmly smiled in our direction.

Our waiter, Alex, practiced his seldom-used English on us, which made everyone feel comfortable; but we let Vinnie do all the talking when it came to ordering.

We didn't know what to expect, but afterwards we all agreed: BEST. ITALIAN. MEAL. EVER.

PERIOD.

Forget about Mario Batali. Giada who? Better than the North End of Boston. Even better than Mamma makes (with all due respect to my wife's cooking and her mother's as well).

Owner Giuseppe Trimboli brought out all types of *antipasti*, then entrée after entrée, plus fresh-baked bread like we had never tasted before this magical night. The *vino della casa* (house wine) flowed freely.

The pasta selections were served in an unusual, but very logical, presentation on concave roof tiles layered with aluminum foil that kept the pasta very hot and somehow even more delicious than we could expect.

The starters included: marinated mushrooms; beans and greens; capocollo (cured pork cold cut) with goat cheese; shredded carrots;

roasted peppers and potatoes (my favorite); crostini; stuffed zucchini; fried mozzarella; stuffed eggplant; shredded cabbage; and marinated zucchini. I exaggerate not. The quantity sufficed as enough for two meals; the quality as once in a lifetime.

Main dishes were ravioli stuffed with parmesan cheese, ham, veal, and tomato; pasta with porcini mushrooms; and *bistecca* (steak). For dessert we had *profiterole* (creamy chocolate cream puffs), hazelnut *canastrelli* (cookies), *sfogliatelle* (flaky pastry), and, of course, tiramisu. Once we finished our wine, we consumed *amaro*, a bitter digestive liqueur, and our old standby, limoncello.

By the time we returned to the hotel it was nearly midnight. We kept our windows open and the sea breeze carried in the soothing sounds of the waves of the Ionian Sea lapping the shore directly across the street like a lullaby. We were in deep sleep within minutes.

•

Somewhere over the Atlantic a few years later after a subsequent trip to Italy, we happened to be seated near a man from Calabria. We told him that we had stayed in a tiny resort town on the Ionian seacoast called Marina di Gioiosa Ionica.

The man's face lit up in acknowledgment. Gioiosa, it turned out, was near to his own hometown. He now lived in New York with his family who were seated in the row in front of him.

"We had the meal of our lives in Calabria," I said to Mr. Lombardo in my best Italian. At that point one of the man's teenage daughters turned around in her seat and asked in perfect English, "Where?"

"In a restaurant situated on top of a hill town, Martone, that is so small there is no need to even paint a sign on the *trattoria*, since it is the only one in town, and why waste the paint we were told," I answered.

The daughter replied in a self-satisfied tone, "You won't believe this, but we just ate at that same restaurant yesterday. That is indeed the best restaurant in Calabria. We beg my father to eat there every year when we visit."

Pit Tip: Although speed limits may at times seem to be non-existent, 130 kilometers per hour is the top speed (110 when it's raining). Travel at speeds at which you feel comfortable and keep one eye glued on your rearview mirror at all times for flashing headlights of oncoming speeders. Some may be going upwards of well over a hundred miles an hour! When they do approach, just pull over to the right as quickly as possible. Otherwise, they may actually bump a "slow" (80 mph) vehicle for intimidation purposes.

Upon reaching a hotel, keep in mind that your elevator may run at a snail's pace and electricity might not come on until you activate it. And on that note, always try to imagine the least likely places for light switches in hotel rooms as well as in the elevators. That just may be where you will find them.

Pit Tip: If you are ever in Calabria, you must find Martone and its hole-in-the-wall restaurant, but remember that its name, La Collinetta, will not be painted on the building, because everyone in Martone already knows about it, so why waste any paint?

Pit Tip: Never hesitate to make small talk with a stranger. The theory of six degrees of separation proves correct even on international flights. It served to validate our wonderful Martone dining experience and to make new friends at the same time.

CHAPTER SIX

Taking Your Car on the Ferry

(Sicily)

As Goethe once advised: "To have seen Italy without having seen Sicily is not to have seen Italy at all, for Sicily is the clue to everything."

And so, after our amazing meal, Jean, Joe, Jackie, and I headed to the island, intending to explore for a few days. Although we had not planned it, Vinnie ended up hitching a ride with us. He had a wedding in Taormina to attend, and because his car was in the shop for repairs, we offered him a one-way ride. He would take the train, ferry, and another train for the return trip.

The drive from Gioiosa Marina to the city of Reggio Calabria at the toe of Italy presented us with a high-altitude adventure. Vinnie told us that the one stretch of *autostrada* we were on near the coast was the highest point in the Italian highway system above open air below us. Looking straight ahead was fine, but as we stole glances over to the right, we knew he was telling the truth. The sight of the drop down left us breathless.

Once at the port we were glad we had Vinnie direct us to the private ferry, which he knew from experience was faster and more efficient than the public one; it also ran more frequently, which mean a shorter waiting time. We drove our car onto the ferry and sailed across the Strait of Messina to Sicilia, the land of Jackie's ancestors, with much excitement, wondering what surprises the largest island in the Mediterranean would offer.

We dropped Vinnie off at the church for the wedding, but unfortunately he was too late for the ceremony. We did get to briefly meet the newlyweds, however. As we left Vinnie with his friends, he told us to be sure to call him to make dinner plans.

Driving up the steep mountainside upon which Taormina rests, I attempted several times to find our hotel, maneuvering the narrow streets, dodging tourists and cars coming at us from all directions. I actually made three hair-raising, round trips up and down the steep hillside before we found the hidden road with Hotel Villa Viadoro. It was worth all of the confusion: our balcony, which overlooked the pool, afforded us a spectacular vista of the Ionian Sea and Mt. Etna, topped off with clouds, hazy in the distance.

Attempting to describe one of the most beautiful places in the world is like struggling to comprehend the Theory of Relativity. Mere everyday words cannot produce the answer. Like Einstein writing a complex formula on a blackboard with a combination of several math symbols, a blank slate, and a few pieces of chalk in a variety of colors, a writer would need to become a virtual artist in order to depict this quintessential Baroque resort city as if he were painting it on a canvas. Perhaps the best way I can express this panoramic setting is that Jackie and I decided that Taormina is where we want our ashes to be spread someday.

We sauntered through narrow alleyways and pedestrian concourses, passing by quaint shops and restaurants. Just walking the streets of Taormina leaves you in awe. Its detailed architecture features gargoyles and wrought iron balconies overflowing with decorative pots containing ruby red bougainvillea and multi-colored birds of paradise. A stroll through the public gardens reveals other exotic specimens.

One of the hotels even features an integrated funicular that takes sunbathers down the hillside to its splendid beach.

Standing atop the skeletal remains of the acoustically perfect Greco-Roman amphitheater offers unbelievable vistas, making this spectacular ancient dig one of the most precious jewels in all of Italy.

While still archeologically considered a ruin, this venue continues to host concerts with the addition of temporary stages and seating. Seeing the azure coastline far below us and a few faint flumes emitting from Mt. Etna in the distance, we realized that the ancestors of Taormina's residents had the same desires and creativity to appreciate a magnificent, aesthetic site as would leading contemporary architects.

We spotted a handsome-looking bridal couple posing for their photographs in the public gardens and seized the opportunity to take pictures of their cute flower girl and shy ring bearer as they awaited their turn with the professional photographer. It was not the wedding of Vinnie's friends, but little did we know that we, too, were about to end up at that reception.

When we had called Vinnie mid-afternoon from our hotel, he asked exactly where we were staying, and he realized we were just a ten-minute walk from the restaurant where the reception was being held.

Without consulting the celebrating couple, he unilaterally invited us to join in the festivities.

Minutes later, we delighted in finding them under colorful umbrellas shading the terrace of the Ristorante del Duomo, which faces the main piazza of Taormina. The newlyweds had chosen to host a small, intimate affair with only thirty or so family members and guests, but you would have thought we were long-lost relatives the way everyone welcomed us. Despite the fact that we were wearing Bermuda shorts and casual clothes, nothing mattered more than our presence as special international guests. The circumstances surrounding our invitation reminded me of a biblical wedding parable in which guests failed to don appropriate nuptial garments upon being called from the street to attend.

I soon found myself offering a toast to the bride and groom who, besides Vinnie, were the only ones who understood English. Glasses were raised and voices in unison saluted the couple with best wishes for a long marriage: *"Cent'anni!"* A hundred years.

Verbalizing that we enjoyed the creamy wedding cake as our midday snack would be an injustice to the most delicious one we have ever tasted (other than our own). The free-flowing *prosecco* was the perfect complement to wash it down. How many other tourists can say that they had been invited to a wedding in romantic Taormina while on vacation? We knew we were lucky and drank in every special moment.

Later we strolled the main pedestrian way, Corso Umberto. We poked our heads into every shop of interest, ranging from art galleries to jewelry shops. We craned our necks to absorb multiple flower-laden window boxes on the second and third stories. We enjoyed hearing the mix of Italian and Germanic voices. The Germans love to vacation here since their historic association with Sicily goes back centuries to Frederick II.

We took a moment to "people-watch" some tourists seated at an umbrella-shaded café checking out other passersby. Later, it being Saturday evening, we chose to go to one of the local parish churches for Mass spoken in Italian since, unfortunately, the *Duomo* (cathedral) did not have a service scheduled.

We did, however, elect to return to that central piazza for dinner at our favorite restaurant in Taormina—the one where we had attended the wedding reception a few hours prior. A wonderful swordfish entrée with capers and olives called *involtini* satisfied our evening hunger. As a bonus attraction, we got to chat again with the owner, Natale, whom we had befriended earlier in the day. Taormina's spell had enveloped us as in a dream world—morning, noon, and night.

Pit Tip: Call your hotel in advance to be sure to get exact driving directions and always be willing and ready to go to an Italian wedding if you are fortunate enough to get invited—even if you're wearing Bermuda shorts.

And remember if you're going to Sicily from the mainland, the private ferry operation from Calabria is faster, more efficient, and runs more frequently than the public one.

CHAPTER SEVEN

Eureka! A Family Reunion

(Siracusa, Sicily)

We drove for about an hour and a half along the autostrada that hugs the Ionian coastline, passing Mount Etna—one of the most active volcanoes in the world—which was shrouded by low-hanging clouds. A brief shower, the first of our trip, danced across our windshield, but the sun returned as we approach Siracusa.

In 734 BC, this city was founded as a colony of Greece and then quickly grew in power and cultural stature, even withstanding an Athenian occupation in the fifth century BC. Famous for its Greek amphitheater ruins, Siracusa was also the birthplace of renowned mathematician Archimedes. He is remembered for his alleged one-word exclamation—"Eureka!"—when he solved the puzzle of King Hiero's gold crown (whether the goldsmith had used solid gold as requested or had mixed in silver) by realizing he could measure the crown's volume by the amount of water it displaced. He figured this out while lowering himself into a full bathtub and seeing water flow over the sides. Fellow mathematician, Pythagoras, had lived and even started a school in nearby Calabria, but their life lines did not intersect because they lived two hundred years apart.

Greek tragedies are still performed at the Teatro Greco, which is one of the most complete standing examples of its kind, and is noted for being acoustically superb. Another notable site in the Archaeological Park of Siracusa is the Ear of Dionysius, a cave with extraordinary auditory attributes, where legend has it that the tyrant of the same name kept his prisoners so that even by their slightest of whispers he could learn of his enemies' plans. A few centuries later, a Roman theater was also carved out of the stone of the hillside and used for circuses and gladiator battles.

Ortygia is the name of the small island that is actually the historical center of Siracusa. Its medieval and Baroque influence is reflected to this day, especially in the presence of the *Duomo*, which is built on the site of a former temple of Athena. An earthquake in 1693 necessitated the entire rebuilding of the area; hence the sculpted gargoyles and mermaids and Baroque architecture featuring ornate cornices and heavy wrought iron balconies laden with gorgeous flowers (as we had seen in Taormina). The Piazza del Duomo is considered one of the most beautiful in all of Italy. In fact, it was chosen as the main venue for an Italian movie set during World War II called *Malèna*.

As the result of our taking a wrong turn after exiting the autostrada, we found ourselves inching our rental down a narrow road that emptied out into this piazza, where we eerily noticed that not one other vehicle was present. Feeling almost naked and fearing we were going to get a ticket for driving in a pedestrian-only area, we quickly found another street leading out of the piazza and breathed a sigh of relief.

Over time, we would come to realize this methodology would be a trend for us: we could always find the city we wanted, but it took us forever to find our hotel. Fortunately, we met up with a young couple walking with their children in strollers. As they responded to our cries of "*scusi,*" the father said, "You don't know how lucky you are to find someone here on a Sunday afternoon who speaks English." They not only gave us good directions that we clearly understood, but they also pointed down the street to a *pasticceria* (pastry shop) where we could buy a dessert tray to take to Jackie's relatives.

Jackie is a connoisseur of licorice, in particular the black anise variety. Thanks to her expertise, on our first trip to Italy in 1998 we wandered the streets of Florence and Venice with a steady supply in our pockets, popping bite-sized pieces into our mouths. We asked the owners of the *pasticerria*— in English—if they carried any flavors of this treat.

"*Non capisco,*" was the owner's reply. He didn't understand.

A little louder now, as if that would make a difference: "Do you have licorice?"

This time the owner and his wife just shrugged their shoulders. Perhaps we should go over to the Ear of Dionysius for better clarity, I thought to myself.

"Candy?"

"*Sì*, candy," the man said as he pointed to candied almonds.

"No. Candy, *nero*, black," I explained. Still, no luck. One more time I slowly pronounced licorice.

This time the light bulb goes off. "*Ah, liquirizia*," the owner said.

We weren't too far off, I thought.

While we were at the store, I asked to use the phone to call Jackie's relatives, but the man insisted on selling me a long distance card to use in the public phone until he realized that we were just trying to make a local call to my wife's family. I told myself that next time I would bring a *telefonino* (cell phone).

We were on our way to meet Jackie's cousin from Connecticut whom we affectionately call "Little Tommy" so as not to confuse him with her father's brother, also named Tommy. As a reservist, Little Tommy often took military "hops" to Italy to visit his relatives. In a gesture beyond normal generosity, he specifically planned his annual trek to Sicily to coincide with our visit so he could be there to translate for everyone. Only we couldn't find the hotel where we were supposed to meet him. Another stop for directions, this time in a restaurant in which the lone patron happened to be an older man from, of all places, Bridgeport, Connecticut (our home state), and then we were on the right track to the Jolly Inn.

Tommy and Jackie's and Tommy's cousin Adolfo, an architect in the neighboring suburb of Solarino, were waiting for us and escorted us to Adolfo's house.

With our tray of *cannoli, cassata* (a Sicilian cake)*,* and various candies, we were welcomed inside to meet Adolfo's wife, Mariella, their adult children, Adolfo's sister, aunts, a brother-in-law, and a niece. It was a three-ring circus with the ladies offering to cook a feast just for us and conversations were flowing in all directions. Smatterings of broken Italian and broken English thinly connected the speakers together momentarily until Tommy could help finish one train of thought for one group and then intercede with another complete translation for someone else. To further complicate communications, Tommy suffers from hearing loss and wears a hearing aid, so we practically had to yell at one another.

After a dish of delicious pasta and our gift of *dolci (sweets)*, Adolfo offered more sedate, philosophical, parting words to us, "Jackie, these are your roots."

Pit Tip: Take the hint from Dionysius and Little Tommy—listen carefully to directions and people who know how to speak both English and Italian loudly and clearly. When speaking and listening in Italian to relatives or to shop owners, however, note that saying things "a little louder" rarely makes any difference. Learning the Italian language wouldn't hurt either; I've studied since then.

Regarding communications, whether you have your own phone set up for European travel or rent or buy one in Italy, just remember to use a Bluetooth device. Don't have the phone in your hand when driving or you'll be fined!

Here is a list of telephone numbers to use in case of an emergency:

12 - Telephone Directory Assistance Number

112 - Carabinieri (Italian National Military Police)

113 - Emergency Police Help Number (also Ambulance and Fire)

115 - Fire Department

116 - Road Assistance from ACI (Italian Automobile Club)

118 - Medical Emergency (Ambulance)

CHAPTER EIGHT

Maps, Signs, & Getting Directions

(Agrigento, Sicily)

The poet Pindar considered Agrigento's "Valley of the Temples," which dates back to 500 BC, "the most beautiful city built by mortal men." The valley, although lower than the rugged mountains surrounding Agrigento, actually sits on a crest so that an observer has a magnificent view of the Mediterranean Sea a few miles below. These Greek ruins, in particular those of the Temple of Concord, represent the best examples of Doric temple architecture still existing in the world today, more so than those in Greece itself. In addition, the brushstrokes of the Divine Artist paint a landscape of an unusual juxtaposition of centuries-old, gnarly olive trees intermingled with almond groves and redolent lemon trees.

During a visit with Jackie's relatives in Siracusa, Sicily, we announced we were headed next for Agrigento. No one, however, had asked us if we knew the most direct way there, which we learned later would have been via autostrada north to Catania, and then the autostrada southwest to the Valle dei Templi. Such a trip should have taken us about two and a half hours, so we didn't worry when setting out just a couple hours before dusk. And anyway, we had gotten that far in the trip with only our trustworthy maps, the same ones that indicated a national highway along the southern coast of Sicily (non-existent to this day); so we set off on our own winding journey with confidence.

The craggy Sicilian countryside has been trampled and deforested for centuries by invaders and locals alike. Yet what remains today still left us intoxicated with its scents and scenes: rock walls a few feet high divide the property lines of farms like tic-tac-toe grids; ubiquitous white *rucola* (arugula) covers nearly every square foot of open land; bucolic remains of stone and wood hovels serve as reminders of poor farmhouses from a few centuries ago.

We had asked for directions to Agrigento at a gas station a few kilometers outside of Siracusa, but we knew we were in trouble when we kept seeing signs for one small town after another, such as Noto. I thought to myself that we probably should have taken that town's name more literally by saying "no to" this route, but we forged ahead and on to the next small town.

We climbed up to the chocolate mecca of Modica, leveled off, and then I wondered aloud why the guidebook stated that the next town, Ragusa, had a great flood that destroyed much of the town, since we saw no low-lying areas. Just then we drew a collective gasp as we found ourselves on another "mile-high" bridge way above the valley where the town rests, recalling our Calabrian drive with Vinnie.

As dusk fell, we were precariously navigating hairpin turns on the edge of a mountainside.

At the exact moment we entered into a particularly sharp "ess" curve, our fate was to meet a huge tour bus heading right at us from around the bend. After expertly avoiding collision and catching his breath, Joe, who had the honor of driving this leg of the journey, exclaimed, "I've been in airplanes that flew at lower altitudes than where we're at right now."

Nightfall brought us to Comiso. Already we had driven a couple of hours into our journey, but convinced we couldn't be too far from our destination, we continued to plod along the coastline, one town at a time. Certain stretches of road were four-lane, while others had but one because of a washout.

Another three hours passed and finally in the middle of the night, we arrived on the outskirts of Agrigento, having seen more of the largest island in the Mediterranean than we had ever anticipated. And we promptly vowed to buy a new map in the morning after our Sicilian breakfast.

•

Like countless travelers before us and many to follow in our tire tracks, we did sometimes manage to get lost—and what better place to get lost than in beautiful Sicily? Somehow, with me at the wheel and Joe navigating, we arrived on the outskirts of Agrigento after nearly five hours of driving from Siracusa where we had visited Jackie's relatives.

Anyone aware of our track record of finding hotels in our destination towns can guess what happened next.

Despite a few stops at stores and government buildings for directions, we found ourselves high on the apex of the town—totally and utterly lost. As much as I hated to do so, once again I pulled over to a carabiniere dressed in military fatigues who was seated in a dark corner of the street. I asked how to return to *il centro* (the town's center), and without having to utter a word of thanks in Italian or English, we obediently followed the direction of his submachine gun.

These attention-getting directions got us back to the Valley of the Temples with a huge double sigh of relief: not only was our journey for the day complete, but that helpful gun-toting militiaman did not fire his weapon at us.

The Hotel Villa Athena—where we were staying—was less than a mile from the Temple of Concordia, the closest ruins and one of the best-preserved Greek temples in all of Europe. That night before retiring, from the terraces of our room (#205—I highly recommend it if you can get it!), we enjoyed the most priceless view of the spectacular spotlighted temple in all its glory.

In the morning we met an archaeologist working at the site, and he explained that Sicilians are people of the world: some short; some tall; some even have blond hair as a result of the Norman conquest. He looked at Jackie and immediately recognized her as having classic Sicilian features and told her so.

He informed us that the Temple of Concordia had eventually become a Christian church, and for that reason, is the most perfect one standing in the Valley of the Temple. Several of the others were in different stages of dismantlement due to the ravages of war and time. We were awestruck to be able to see the ruts made by ancient wagon wheels from 500 BC along the marble ruins that once were their roads.

We spotted a more "modern" vehicle parked nearby: a gaily decorated horse-drawn Sicilian cart that could trace its roots to the days of the Arab invaders as evidenced by the brightly colored festoons and other decorations. Next to this horse and cart, a local octogenarian dressed in native peasant garb stood available for picture-taking. Jackie could not resist mixing with the locals, so we ponied up and paid for her to pose with him. It made for a lovely keepsake photo, but we were definitely glad we didn't have to travel around Sicily in that mode of transportation.

Pit Tip: Get yourself a good map or three of the areas where you plan to drive (or cough up a bunch of euros for a GPS). Speak a little Italian, if you can, and be ready for a flurry of directions.

Memorize the following words: *sinistra* (left), *destra* (right), *vicino* (nearby), *lontano* (far away), *est* (east), *ovest* (west), *nord* (north), and *sud* (south).

Regarding road signs, if a sign with the name of a city points to either the left or right, or both, it invariably means go straight ahead. Blue signs point to cities and towns, white to airports or local attractions, and green heads you in the direction of the autostrada. Brown signs indicate historic, cultural, artistic, and ecological points of interest. Black ones point to industrial areas.

Similar to signs in the US, yellows mean detour, road work, or alternative routes.

Pit Tip: Pulling over to ask directions for how to reach the Valley of the Temples can make a person find religion fast, especially if the person offering help simply points a submachine gun toward the correct road. That's an internationally recognized language without having to utter a word of Italian, English, or Greek.

As an aside, don't be in a hurry to put your cart before the horse in Agrigento. Stay and linger in this classical Greek setting to absorb the civilizations that have passed through, and if you can glimpse the temples lit up at night, all the better.

CHAPTER NINE

Airport Reconnaissance

(Palermo, Sicily)

Upon departing Agrigento and the Valley of the Temples, we headed northward to our next stop, Palermo, or more specifically, its suburban oceanside resort, Mondello. During our drive alongside the craggy mountains, we passed a few tempting signs directing us to cities with readily recognizable names such as Sambuca, Marsala, and the ominous-sounding Corleone of *The Godfather* fame, but we steered clear and stayed the course, saving those for another journey.

Within a couple hours we started to approach the majestic views of Palermo, hugging the rugged coastline. When historians say that Palermo was once the intellectual capital of southern Europe and the crossroads of civilization, their claim is corroborated by the fact that the following cultures have been absorbed into Palermo's art, food, and people: Phoenicians, Carthaginians, Romans, Normans, Arabs,

Swabians, and the Aragonese from Spain. The result is an exotic, thriving big city with a more recently vilified reputation that the people and government today strive to wash clean. The Bay of Mondello sits in the shadow of the massive outcropping of Mt. Pellegrino, which dramatically overlooks the pristine shoreline.

We had enough time to check in at the Mondello Palace Hotel, grab a bite to eat, and then take a stroll through their gardens to the private beachfront (still a little cool, though, for going into the water since it was early November). Soon it was mid-afternoon, and since we planned on leaving the hotel around five o'clock the next morning, we wanted to feel comfortable finding the airport in the predawn darkness. We also wanted to learn the procedure for returning our cherry-red Alfa Romeo at the rental counter at such an early hour of the day. So we set off for the airport, and within a little over an hour were already headed back to the hotel, having completed our logistical mission. We drove and later walked for a closer look around the nearby neighborhoods filled with several blocks of walled stucco estates ensconced with tall palm trees and exotic flowers.

American tourists often find it difficult to wait until eight at night when restaurants typically open in Italy; and it is not atypical for my travel companions and me to be hungry even before that time. Lucky for us, we spotted a *trattoria* outside of downtown Palermo that had just opened for business at sunset.

We felt destined to eat at this place called La Cascina, so we headed in and were quickly seated.

We started to eye our menus, the people, and our surroundings.

Jackie, glancing at one of the waiters, said, "Do you think he looks like—?"

"Yes, he definitely does," responded Jean before my wife could finish her thought. Joe and I took a look, did a double-take, and quickly concurred without a doubt.

With a chuckle to egg me on, Joe said, "John, tell him he does. You speak a bit of Italian."

So before our handsome Italian waiter with the high forehead, thick wavy dark brown hair, and toothy smile could take our orders, I used my very best combination of high school Latin and a few words I had just learned on our vacation, and bluntly but politely said: "*Scusi, signore. Sua . . . er . . . faccia . . . simile . . . er . . . John Kennedy, Jr.*"

He beamed with a broad smile of appreciation and modestly replied, "*Grazie.*"

We four also beamed, proud of our astuteness in recognizing the strong resemblance and for making the effort to compliment him.

"John-John" proceeded to bring us his own compliments—specials of the house, some of which were unique to the Palermo region: a chickpea croquette called *panelle,* plus *crostini* (small bits of toasted bread with various toppings), zucchini, and assorted *assaggi caldi* (hot appetizers), all of which we washed down with a local red wine recommended by the "reincarnated" Kennedy. (Author's Note: To this day, we have never received our American Express charge from La Cascina, and we want to think we know the reason why: our JFK, Jr. look-alike waiter and friend.)

We awoke the next morning to the wind dramatically causing

the long sheer curtains to billow through the casement windows in the hotel rooms and hallways, accompanied by the sound of distant thunder.

Since we couldn't afford to miss our flight from Palermo to Rome, we rushed through the routine of packing our car one last time and headed to the airport, grateful that we had plotted out the way the day before. Fortunately, the storm quickly subsided, but it only added to the beauty, mystery, and aura that surrounded our Sicilian visit. As Frederick II of Hohenstaufen once boasted: "God would not have chosen Palestine if he had seen my kingdom of Sicily." We were inclined to agree.

Pit Tip: If you're not sure where the airport and car rental return are located, try to schedule in a practice run the day before if possible. If not, be prepared to pack in a hurry so you can handle all the logistics involved in getting to the airport and the rental car return on time, especially in the event of stormy weather. It's well worth the effort up front in order to save time and avoid the possibility of missing a flight.

Unrelated to driving but always good advice: Play a hunch and don't be shy about speaking to your waiter. It could pay dividends.

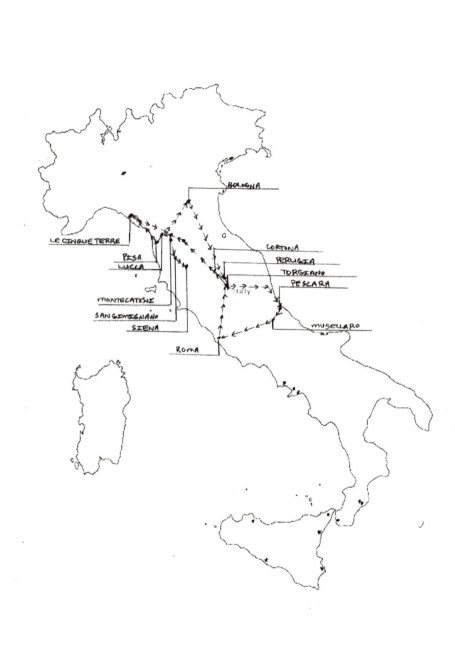

BOLOGNA

LE CINQUE TERRE

CORTONA
PERUGIA
TORGIANO
PESCARA

PISA
LUCCA

Italy

MONTECATINI

SAN GIMIGNANO

MUSELLARO

SIENA

ROMA

PART II

ANOTHER SPIN AROUND ITALY, NOW WITH OFFSPRING!

CHAPTER TEN

Shifting Gears & One-Lane Road Right of Way

(Torgiano, Umbria)

A few years after that trip, Jackie and I—along with our adult son Jay—encountered unanticipated snow showers, paradoxically, as we drove southward on the *autostrada*. The mid-October weather phenomenon occurred because the trip down to Umbria is through the multi-tunneled Apennines and on high overpasses far above valleys below. All this scenery, despite the gray day, captivated Jay on his Italian debut as he helped us navigate and translate the road signs.

The overnight, non-stop scenario of crossing the Atlantic drained us so much that we chose to temporarily bypass Florence, Jackie's favorite city, until we were back in that area later in the week.

Jackie, a self-confessed chocoholic, also agreed to forego the opportunity to catch the tail-end of the International Chocolate Festival in Perugia.

Meanwhile, for our roadside entertainment, Jay used this occasion of skirting Florence to give us a quick language lesson. He explained how words in Italian with the consecutive letters "f-i" convert to "f-l" in English. Firenze and Florence, for example, as well as *fiore*/flower and *fiume*/flume (both mean river).

Through October snow, we drove ten more kilometers deeper into the idyllic Umbria countryside where we expected to find our hotel, Le Tre Vaselle ("The Three Vessels"—but with five stars) nestled in tiny Torgiano.

This classic Italian town-and-country setting with Etruscan roots features a medley of vineyards and olive tree groves with a seven-hundred-year-old stone defense tower overlooking it all. The populated, non-agricultural area consists primarily of several well-restored seventeenth-century brick buildings, including, as we soon learned, our hotel.

We proceeded to enter the heart of Torgiano. The layout of this *comune* (town) is comprised of about half a dozen main streets, each a few blocks long. They all run fairly parallel to one another with alternating one-way traffic.

We spotted a sign for our hotel and I quickly downshifted to make a sharp uphill U-turn. Just as we neared our destination, we were unable to cut the next thirty-degree corner and found ourselves facing a building with not enough room to maneuver between the conjoined streets. The only option was to put the car into reverse.

The last time I had driven a stick shift also happened to be with a rental car in Italy several years earlier. I have also owned a few manual shift cars, so I told myself: "No problem!"

Our five-speed Fiat rental car, however, said, "Problem!" and refused to go into reverse as I pushed down and drew the stick toward me. In fact, it felt as if it would snap if I forced it any further. Like Pagliacci, I was laughing on the outside at my ineptness but secretly crying on the inside.

Deep breath. Get a grip, John, and get this car turned around. After a couple of panicky tries that seemed to take forever, Jay came to the rescue. He realized that not only is the driver supposed to push down and pull back on the stick, but at the same time, pull up the black rubber cushion just below the knob to prevent accidentally shifting into fourth gear.

Fortunately, it was late Sunday afternoon and Torgiano traffic was almost non-existent, so we enjoyed a sigh of "comic" relief as I reversed the car and we headed, finally, to the hotel.

•

As we enjoyed our full breakfast of yogurt, juices, cereals, omelets and breads in the winterized garden terrace of our hotel, we noticed fog on the mountains in the distance. These were the same mountains we would need to cross to reach the Adriatic coast and the Abruzzo region. Our maps indicated a route down the autostrada toward Rome and then eastward, which happened to be several miles longer. Since the time difference was supposedly negligible, we again decided to take the more picturesque route.

After the first half-hour of driving in the valley past Assisi and Foligno, we began our ascent over the Apennines via those back roads. The higher we went, the more curves, drop-offs, and trucks, not to mention BMWs, were anxious to pass us as we kept our car in lower gears for the most part. We were in as remote an area as could be with no sign of modern amenities. Ruddy-faced farmers drove tractors from village to village, which were somehow carved out of the lesser hills and dales. We were soon on the edge of the road as it criss crossed sky-high above the valleys, almost as breathtaking as the Amalfi Coast, lacking only the deep blue Tyrrhenian Sea below it.

We somehow managed to get stuck behind a tanker truck, so the going was even slower than it had been, and then as we approached a small rural community, we came to a complete stop. The reason: a single traffic light determined which direction of traffic would flow through the main street, so narrow it could accommodate only one lane of vehicles. If you lived there and the front door of your house opened outward (which I doubted it would) you would risk getting it and yourself clipped by a passing car or truck.

Eventually, we began to descend and approach the exit for the city of Macerata, internationally renowned for its two-month outdoor opera festival. Unfortunately, we would miss this unique summertime presentation by several months on this trip, but *mai dire mai* (never say never) for the future, we've learned.

Once we reached the coast, captivating views of the Adriatic on our left and snow-capped mountains to the southeast on our right greeted us, and we continued on to Abruzzo.

Pit Tip: It is an absolute must that the renter knows how to drive a stick shift, including how to get it into reverse. Note that the vast majority of rental cars available in Italy are not automatic transmissions, so if you don't know how to drive a stick shift, it is crucial that you book your rental in advance and specifically request an automatic.

And remember: never, never, never pass up an opportunity to savor *cioccolato* (chocolate) in Perugia.

Pit Tip: When is a short cut not a short cut? When it's a long cut, or in a few instances, a very narrow cut. If looking at a map and knowing that the Apennine Mountains need to be crossed, the adventurous driver would choose the winding back roads that appear as if a child has scribbled them in.

Indeed, my travel philosophy is to select the Robert Frost option, the road less traveled by, since the experience can be worth the longer drive time and you may even get a glimpse of everyday farm life or little-known piece of history in Italy. Just because an area may not be featured in the latest travel magazines doesn't mean it's not worth discovering, and you'll likely have a story to tell about your driving itinerary that none of your fellow travelers or friends has experienced.

CHAPTER ELEVEN

Family Reunion *Numero Tre*

(Musellaro, Abruzzo)

As we neared the highway exit for Musellaro, we each experienced a bit of stage fright. I wondered if I could remember the way to the town. What would the relatives we didn't meet in our visit several years ago be like?

Jay's head was spinning with Italian vocabulary and grammar, aware that the pressure was on him to perform as translator.

Jackie worried if the three shawls she had knitted for cousin Gino's wife, Filomena, and his two sisters, Laurina and Santina, would be liked and acceptable. How would they compare to the quality of knitting done locally?

We followed winding roads up the mountain, looking for a *pasticceria* to buy some desserts, but the stores in the village of Bolognano were closed for the afternoon *pausa* (rest), and we doubted one existed in the even smaller Musellaro farther up the mountainside. Fortunately, we found a coffee bar that was open and we bought a box of chocolate candies, so we would not make a *brutta figura* (bad impression) by arriving empty-handed.

Food is paramount in Italy and goes hand-in-driving-glove with family gatherings. We no sooner arrived at Gino's summer-to-fall apartment in Musellaro than the other relatives started to appear. While we were being introduced, Filomena disappeared "backstage" into her tiny kitchen where she began to produce the type of meal usually reserved only for a holiday, as we learned later from Gino's eldest son Dino.

Jackie and I immediately discerned distinct resemblances between Dino and my deceased father: broad forehead; dark wavy hair; pleasant, laid-back personality. He had taken the afternoon off from his consulting business. His wife and teenage children were unfortunately unable to attend.

Gino, who looked good for eighty-four despite some foot and rib injuries experienced in a recent fall, sat proudly in his simple wooden kitchen chair, introducing the rest of his family. His sisters— Laurina, eighty-three, and Santina, seventy-six—had not lost a step in their spry movements since we last saw them. While the sisters and Filomena graciously accepted the hand-knitted shawls from Jackie, I got a polite slap on the cheek from Santina for not having become fluent in Italian.

Gino and Filomena's daughter Anna Maria, her husband, and their teenage son and pre-teen daughter arrived after school. Claudia, whom we had met years before, was there with her dog Leila. Marco, the professor, was unable to make the occasion, which was disappointing because I really wanted to meet him as a fellow writer.

The last son/cousin we met was named Gianni. When we heard his name pronounced, it struck Jay and me the same way. Now I could count four of us who have walked on this planet with my name: my dad, myself, Jay (whose real name is John), and Gianni. Although Gianni looked more like a cousin of mine in the US than my father, his given name combined with Dino's features created strong emotions for me. Gianni worked for the postal system in an internet technology capacity and was accompanied by his wife, a dentist.

Communications were going well. Jay was complimented for his accent and ability to translate both ways, except once when he asked if the dog was a "*ragazza*" (girl) or a "*ragazzo*" (boy). The relatives, including the children, snickered, because in Italian the gender of an animal is described simply as either as male (*maschio) or female (femmina*), but never as a girl or a boy. Dino and Gianni recalled their English enough to explain this little malapropism and later to fill in a few other communication gaps.

However, the best way to overcome any language barrier in Italy is with food, which started to arrive in crescendos from *la cucina* (kitchen), preceded by the tantalizing aromas of rosemary, basil, and oregano.

Prosciutto and melon and cured sausages were appetizers. Then we enjoyed a delicious *caprese* salad of fresh tomatoes, mozzarella, and basil dressed with olive oil and salt. Next we got into the pasta dishes: a large slice of cheese lasagna and on the same plate, *tagliatelle*, flat and almost half-inch wide pasta tossed in a meat sauce. It was so good that I immediately responded "*Sì*" when asked if I want another serving, thinking, quite mistakenly, that this was the main event.

A few minutes later, out came breaded chicken cutlets, which melted in our mouths. Once we consumed those, we savored some fried cheese shaped like meatballs, only better tasting. These were soon followed by a serving of *braciola*, thin beefsteak rolled and stuffed with minced garlic, parsley, and parmesan cheese. Baked chicken and roasted potatoes were the next delicacy.

Where was all this food coming from? And more importantly, where was I going to put it? We still had to eat pickled cauliflower for a vegetable as well as salad greens, both of which were sitting in dishes on the table waiting for us.

Finally, dessert (as if we needed it) arrived. It included fruit, a cheese-filled *torta* (cake), and a few chocolate-hazelnut candies.

We complimented Filomena not only on the various tastes, but also for her magic in preparing such a feast in so small a kitchen, in such a short period of time.

During a *passeggiata* (walk) around the village with the younger relatives after our banquet, Dino and Gianni stopped to point out an empty lot and foundation, and next to it, the remains of a deserted stone hovel, overgrown with tall weeds and small wild trees. After a brief, slightly heated discussion in Italian between themselves, they came to an agreement. They explained to us that these respective plots of land represented the two domiciles of my grandfather, his family, and their livestock when he was a youngster back in the late 1800s. In essence, as descendants, we were all part owners of this little piece of heaven adjacent to the castle walls with a bucolic view fit for a king, overlooking the Parco Nazionale d'Abruzzo, the Abruzzo National Park.

For a few moments, time stood still as Jackie and I pondered if we should build on this property some day and have our own place under the Abruzzo sun. A reverse migration after a couple of generations.

Mai dire mai . . . .

Pit Tip: Visiting your relatives in the Old Country can sometimes be like looking in a mirror. You'll see characteristics, traits, and nuances of yourself and other immediate family members in the cousins, aunts, and uncles who live overseas. While you are visiting, enjoy the **abbondanza** (abundance) of Italian cuisine! You can go on a diet before you travel to Italy or when you return.

Above all, when traveling in Italy, keep an open mind. You never know what adventure might be waiting for you, especially if you choose less traveled roads.

CHAPTER TWELVE

Toll Booth

(Arezzo, Tuscany)

After our family reunion, we found our way down another winding mountainside to the autostrada, headed in the direction of Rome. We still had to cross the Apennines, but at least we were on the highway, a straight shot through the lighted tunnels inside the mountains instead of having to go around them on the dangerous, and now dark, curves of the back roads' route we had taken that morning.

A few hours later, we stopped at an *Autogrill, the designated place to make a "pit stop" on Italian highways,* northeast of Rome to change drivers—and a funny thing happened on our way to the Forum.

In the parking lot, we noticed some Japanese tourists taking turns posing next to a Lamborghini. Thinking it was a great idea for a photo op, I decided to wait my turn to do the same. So there I was looking my jet-setter best, leaning against this lavish red sports car, when out of the rest area's convenience store/restaurant strode the Italian owner. Fortunately, I had just flashed a smile for the camera, so I just continued grinning sheepishly at him—my way of acknowledging and complimenting his beautiful car while stealthily backpedaling away from it.

Inside, my "luck" continued. While most people were buying bottled water, panettone, torrone, CDs, etc., I was fascinated by a miniature bottle of Coca-Cola with a most unusual handle resembling a musical G clef. Being an Atlantan who had never seen such a Coke bottle, I mused that it would make a great conversation piece for my office. The only question mark was whether this fragile handle would withstand the pressure within my suitcase. Was it plastic or glass?

Only one way to test it. I put some finger pressure on it and . . . oops! Splashing Coca-Cola on my white sweatshirt, I quickly learned the hard way that it was glass. The disgusted clerk merely shook his head, but, mercifully did not charge me the $14 for the broken Coke bottle. Also fortunately, I did not get hurt, only my pride.

We quickly hopped back into our car, and I took over as navigator while Jay drove on the A1 northward toward Perugia and Firenze. I was doing my best to match the obscure, tiny, indecipherable village dots on the map with our favorite new Italian word-of-the-day: *uscita* (meaning "exit" and pronounced with a soft "sh" sound). Along this same highway, upon our arrival to Italy heading south, the Perugia *uscita* had been clearly marked; I mistakenly assumed the same going northbound.

That night, however, none of the somewhat larger cities were referenced on the road signs, although I could sense we were getting close just by the amount of time we had driven. It was coming on 11 pm, so we called my relatives in Musellaro, whom we had just visited, to tell them we were okay.

Soon, in a tone of frustration for not being able to find the right exit and out of total exhaustion, Jackie's mezzo-soprano voice from the back seat set up a duet between her and me, but we were not singing a lullaby—though our son did scold us for acting like *bambini* (children) as we bickered about exits and directions.

Suddenly, I spotted an exit indicating Arezzo, which I remembered was north of Perugia. On this note, our serious drama turned comedic opera as I yelled to Jay: "*Uscitaaaaa!* We've gone past Perugia! We need to take this *uscita*—now!"

This toll station had two booths, and we choose the automated one. Upon sliding the toll ticket into the slot, Jay learned that we owed twenty euros and twenty cents (about twenty-six, hard-earned American dollars at the time), which I handed to him. A small cup opened up on the machine and he placed the bill and the coin in it, then he shut it. In that same split second that it retracted, we all realized that the toll gate was not rising because that cup was for coins only and my twenty-euro note was not going to be digested by the coin slot.

As cars pulled in behind us, then impatiently maneuvered their way out of our line into the next lane, what did Jackie do but start to laugh in disbelief. Jay saw no humor in this plot nor did I. A foreign voice began to crackle through the squawk box, and Jay responded with a clear Italian accent, but being flustered, totally wrong grammar:

"I need to help myself, please." He realized the inanity of it and quickly corrected himself to say that he needed the man to help him.

Next thing we knew the gate opened and we started to pull away, but the toll master was waving us down from behind. Jay stopped the car, got out, and walked back to speak to the man in charge. Jay started to explain that *"mia madre"* (my mother) was involved and the man immediately empathized with him.

Without speaking another word, but with many Italian hand signals, he instructed the next driver to insert his toll ticket, thus forcing the coin box to re-open where my twenty euro note, fortunately, was still resting. Since the money could not be used for that next driver's toll, and since the toll collector apparently had no way to record a cash transaction inside his office, and quite possibly because he felt badly for Jay's mother, he handed the note back to Jay and waved him away with a pleasant, *"Ciao!"*

Whether it was simply Italian hospitality or Italian bureaucracy at its finest or a mix of both, we landed up with our twenty-six dollar admission charge back in our pocket.

We were shocked, delighted—and still lost. Our version of *A Night at the Opera* was not yet over.

After a couple of false turns, we spotted a *carabiniere* (military police officer) vehicle with two officers who had pulled someone over. I started to get out to ask for directions, but was summarily waved back into our car with the point of a submachine gun until they settled with the other driver. I obeyed immediately, of course. Apparently, however, they were just giving the driver a speeding ticket, and we only had to wait for a few minutes.

The police were truly friendly. They directed us back on the highway—heading south—since it was the faster way to our hotel rather than the unlit back roads. We arrived back in Torgiano not too long after that.

Pit Tip: Don't squeeze the charming souvenirs. Only pack wine or olive oil in your suitcase if you are a very high risk-taker and/or protect the bottles extremely well.

And, whenever possible, try not to get too close to anyone's Lamborghini, Maserati, Ferrari, or you might get run over by the owner. Or at least get flashed a hairy eyeball.

Pit Tip: Given a choice between a toll booth with an operator or an automated one, go with the live person. Your chances of ever getting a free toll pass have virtually evaporated since my family and I hit the one-in-a-trillion jackpot with our "slot machine" caper.

And don't worry should a ***carabiniere*** ever point a gun at you to give directions. He or she will typically be quite friendly, so just do as they say, follow the directions as indicated by the weapon, and you shouldn't have to worry about them writing a ticket.

CHAPTER THIRTEEN

Driving Under the Tuscan Sun

(Cortona, Tuscany)

Jay took us and the Fiat up and around switchbacks and curves to *the center of town*. We were fortunate to have made arrangements to meet with an eminent guide in Cortona: Professor C. Parker Robinson. He's better known to us as "Chris," a contemporary of Jay's, friend and former neighbor from when we lived in South Carolina. After Frances Mayes, bestselling author of *Under the Tuscan Sun*, he is probably one of the best-known Americans, or at least Georgia-born Americans, living in this hill town of Tuscany.

Although we had not seen Chris for a number of years, and even though he was sporting a wispy beard and Italian-style eyeglasses to add to his persona, we recognized him immediately as if we had just seen him the prior week.

He had perfected his Italian accent living in Tuscany over the past six years while working as an instructor of pottery at the University of Georgia Studies Abroad Program. (Author's Note: Professor Robinson is currently the Director of the entire UGA program in Cortona.) Although other fine arts such as paper-making and marble-sculpting are also part of the curriculum, Chris has put ceramics to the forefront. He organized a unique collection of medieval pottery from a museum in Rome (adding his interpretations of these ceramic designs, using similar classical techniques) and hosted the exhibit in the Museum of Cortona. Local officials have recognized him for all of his contributions.

Therefore we were not surprised when, prior to meeting up with Chris, we walked into a gift shop and the English-speaking proprietor, Alessandra, said she knew him. Likewise, when we did rendezvous with Chris at the *Caffè degli Artisti* for espresso, before I could buy him a cup, a local acquaintance has already offered him one. The *barista* struck up the incomparable cacophony of the coffeemaker faster than a Ferrari at Monza (Italy's most famous race track) and nearly as loud. It was a moment straight out of Frances Mayes' books in which she describes the congeniality of the residents who are always taking turns buying espresso for her, her husband, and one another.

As we caught up on news with Chris, Jay was composing questions as to how he might be able to land a job working in Italy and become as proficient in Italian as Chris was. They promised to stay in touch via e-mail on this subject.

Chris led us down a pedestrian-friendly main street when, almost on cue, strains of a melody being sung by renowned Italian tenor Andrea Bocelli wafted from a shopkeeper's doorway. We turned left and proceeded up a steeply pitched street for half a mile to the UGA campus. Chris had no problems making the grade. We managed pretty well this time but realized you really have to have the lungs of a *basso profondo* and the legs of a soccer player (*calciatore*), to do this climb as well as several others on a daily basis. As we paused to study the view, an elderly lady, who had also just made the grade without a problem, passed by.

The campus hosts fifty students and has a staff of about fifteen professors that run the programs. The town and gown officials have contracted for the university to use a historical convent/nursing home for the classroom building. Chris introduced us to the students at work in various classes. He culminated the tour in his studio where he modestly showed us examples of his artistry. As we reviewed the program for the exhibit he managed, we noted a distinct resemblance to the styles of several hundred years ago. We gave him "bravos" for his work and thanked him for his private excursion.

We descended back to the main piazza via another street as Chris pointed out a thirteenth century church built by an associate of St. Francis of Assisi. As a knowledgeable local, Chris also pointed out the more ordinary facets of town life such as the type of apartment where his parents would stay during their Christmas visit; a good angle from which we should take a picture of a particularly inviting alleyway; and where the post office was located. Most importantly, he gave us driving directions to "*Bramasole*," the charming home of Frances Mayes—a must-see for all American sightseers.

It was a damp, overcast day so we treated Chris and ourselves to a hearty lunch of *ribollita*, a thick, Tuscan specialty soup featuring beans, vegetables, and bread. Add Parmesan cheese, drizzle extra-virgin olive oil over it and you have native comfort food that fills and warms your stomach. Afterward, we told him "*grazie mille*" (a thousand thanks) for his time and wished him "*buona fortuna*" (good luck).

Jackie was on a high note as we scaled the Cortona hilltop even farther in search of the special estate and started to take in even more inspiring, breathtaking views of the valley. Then she exhaled in disappointment as we had to turn around after fifteen minutes of futilely looking for the charmingly aged, pink stucco villa.

Just as we were re-approaching the edges of the commercial district, she homed in on a restaurant and immediately took control of the situation. She exited the car, crossed the street, and rehearsed in her mind a monologue in her best Italian. She politely asked the merchant for directions to the famous landmark: "*Per piacere, dov⊠è Bramasole?*"

The woman proprietor responded in mock exasperation and in perfect English: "You are the millionth person today to ask for those directions and you are the last one I am going to help."

It turned out that this was the exact *strada, street,* we needed to be on and Bramasole was about a mile down the road. We drove a short distance and Jackie spotted the roadside grotto adorned with fresh flowers, just as she remembered from Mayes' books.

"Stop the car!" she commanded. "This is it."

We got out and approached a driveway protected by a large wrought-iron gate. Through the fence we admired the re-built, moss-speckled Etruscan walls and the beautiful seasonal landscaping —but no house. However, when we turned around, we realized the driveway did not face the direction of the *bella casa, beautiful house.* There, high above a cluster of silver-and-sage-colored olive trees, proudly sat the totally renovated Bramasole.

Jackie extemporaneously decided to strike the pose of a *prima donna* leaning against the stone-and-mortar gatepost, while Jay played *paparazzo* (celebrity photographer) and began snapping pictures. Jackie's dream as owner of an Italian villa appeared to be realized, if only for a few moments.

Pit Tip: Park outside the city center of Cortona and take a day to walk casually and absorb all the beauty of this quintessential hill town.

Also, before your trip, read Frances Mayes' ***Under the Tuscan Sun*** and her other books about Cortona and Tuscany. As a last resort, you can rent the movie of the same name, but it is not even close to telling the real story.

If you decide to go searching for Frances Mayes' famous house, **Bramasole**, stop for directions at the restaurant located on a corner when you drive to the farthest edges of the commercial district. And ask nicely!

CHAPTER FOURTEEN

Parking & Street Racing

(Montecatini Terme, Tuscany)

During the late nineteenth century, Verdi, Puccini, and Ruggiero Leoncavallo, who wrote *Pagliacci,* were known to frequent Montecatini Terme, a popular resort location known since the 1300s for its spas and their curative health benefits. Today a thriving area, quite cosmopolitan, it prides itself with having upscale shopping, hotels, and classic villas interspersed among trees and numerous parks.

Higher on the hilltop rests the lyrically named Montecatini Alto, the Old World town, which is also worth a winding drive and stroll. And so on one of our visits to Italy, Jackie and I set out for this area on a magical musical mystery tour.

We were scheduled to stay at a grande dame, luxury, four-story hotel, and thanks to friendly residents we encountered at an outdoor market and again at a park, we eventually found our way after driving through the darkened streets. When we arrived, our jaws dropped as the structure resembled a once-opulent opera house. We entered the driveway through the main gate of the walled-in, heavily-landscaped grounds and parked our car at the foot of the stairs.

To check-in, we would have to walk up nearly three dozen wide concrete steps flanked by a decorative balustrade on both sides, leading up to the floodlit entranceway. Inside, the lobby showed signs of recent renovation: several Venetian glass chandeliers hanging from its high ceiling, oriental carpets, and a grand staircase with brass railings enhanced the hotel's ambience. As we headed back down the stairway after registering, the theatrical maxim "break a leg" earned new meaning as my bad knee suddenly gave out from under me. I slipped on the wet surface but caught my balance before falling.

Stefano, the ever-present majordomo of the Grand Hotel Vittoria (now defunct), parked our car for us while we carried our suitcases back up the flight of steps.

The next morning we found our rented Fiat in the hotel's basement parking lot. Once buckled up, we somehow managed to figure out the way to activate the buzzer, and then waited thirty seconds for the gate to swing open and let us out. Unfortunately, we hadn't asked for any directions on where to go from there, and so ensued another of our driving adventures.

Some background: "park" in Italian has two different words

attached to its meanings. *Il parcheggio* is a car park or parking lot, whereas *il parco* is a large public green space in a town used for recreation—of which, as I mentioned, there are many in Montecatini Terme. Don't try to combine both words into one definition as I did when I came off the steep ramp of the parking garage toward the street, clutching, braking, shifting, and lurching—all simultaneously—only to land up on the pathway of a pedestrian-only park.

Totally flustered, I committed an even further *brutta figura* by driving through the greensward area as bewildered residents stared at the *pazzo americano*, crazy American. In my (weak) defense, it had appeared to me to be the only route without going the wrong direction on a one-way lane by which I could see us heading toward the city center without getting lost again in the maze of streets of Montecatini Terme.

Wrong.

A couple of nights later near the same park, as pedestrians returned from shopping, we again had to ask for directions to the hotel. Fortunately, the locals were happy to oblige us, and if they recognized us as the municipality's infamous motor vehicle offenders, no one said a word. Thank goodness.

•

We managed to find our hotel a little sooner on our second night in Montecatini Terme. However, after having to go around several blocks, we were still unable to access the little side street for the garage entrance. So we pulled up to the front steps and ascended them to ask for help from Stefano.

A rather portly, middle-aged fellow with an outgoing, teddy-bear personality, Stefano volunteered to drive the car with Jay and myself as passengers while Jackie went to our room. I've observed that many Italian drivers, when they settle in behind the wheel of a car, go through some type of transformation from being the friendliest people on Earth to nearly maniacal Gran Prix racer wannabes.

Stefano was no exception.

After managing to squeeze his all-too-big-frame into our tiny Fiat, he shifted into gear, wheeled the car around in the driveway, squealed out into the street, and proceeded to take us on a ride that rivaled the chase scene in the classic movie, *Bullitt*. Stefano "McQueen" raced down the narrow side streets, picking and choosing the appropriate one-way turns while managing to skip every stop sign.

Flashing his lights as he approached each residential intersection seemed to adequately warn any oncoming drivers that he was on a mission to help us. Never mind that there were vehicles parked on both sides of the darkened streets and a few residents out arm-in-arm for their evening *passeggiata.*

The area was a *zona di silenzio* (quiet zone) so he couldn't use the horn.

We made the circuitous route around the neighborhood blocks in what I imagined was record-breaking time and found the obscure lane between the city park and the hotel parking entrance. When we arrived, Jay and I looked at each other in relief and in disbelief. Would we ever be able to retrace Stefano's route—and at anywhere near that speed?

Pit Tip: While we escaped with only some blushing faces, do avoid driving in a pedestrian-only park. You not only risk getting a ticket, but perhaps even worse, also committing the most dire of Italian sins: the ***brutta figura***.

In the same vein, vocabulary reminder: a ***parco*** is a park, but ***parcheggio*** refers to a parking garage. And a vehicle only belongs in one of them.

Pit Tip: Do not try Stefano's flashing light routine at home or anywhere else, especially in Italy.

Instead, obey ordinary traffic rules and stop when a sign or light indicates to do so. Do not, however, make a right turn on a red light as it is not permitted in Italy.

Also if you happen to like tooting your horn, be sure to watch for the international sign that designates a quiet zone or ***zona di silenzio.***

Pit Tip: If stopped on a hill at a red light or stop sign, put your transmission in neutral and apply your emergency brake. When it's time to go, step on the clutch and shift into first. As you slowly let out the clutch and it engages, release the brake, give the engine a little more gas than usual, and you should be able to avoid drifting backward.

CHAPTER FIFTEEN

Knowing When to Park & Walk

(Lucca & San Gimignano, Tuscany)

Seeing as we would spend a full four nights in Florence, we chose to temporarily bypass that destination so we could get a preview of Lucca (pronounced "Luke-kah") a little farther down the road. We also passed Pistoia, known as "the greenhouse of Italy," with its acres and acres of nurseries.

No wonder nearby Lucca is so lush. With all this greenery readily available thanks to the warm Tuscan sun, the Town Fathers over the centuries have landscaped even their extra-wide ramparts. This walled city has a veritable park planted above its lovely old-town area since its thick walls are wide enough for walking, jogging, and even bicycling. In fact, all of those methods are excellent ways for appreciating Lucca—but not in the rain as we soon found out.

So much precipitation fell the day of our visit, we were practically forced to tour this special place inside our car. This situation gave us a rather unique perspective, trying to negotiate corners only to run out of room because parked cars were practically everywhere, and so we had to drive in reverse back down the length of entire streets. Furthermore, we discovered that Lucca's Roman street grid was only the width of little more than a sidewalk.

What else was special about Lucca? Like all Italian major cities, it has a beautiful cathedral, and this one commemorates St. Martin who once shared his cloak with a beggar. Lucca is also renowned for its big, annual antique fair. Having just missed it, we spotted the multitude of white tents being disassembled.

Drat!

The great opera composer Giacomo Puccini resided in Lucca, and his house today still contains the piano on which he composed his famous final opera, *Turandot*.

Lastly, one of the world's most beloved fairy tale characters has a close connection to this area. Carlo Lorenzini, author of *The Adventures of Pinocchio, used the name* of the suburb of Collodi as his pen name. Lorenzini had spent many summers in Collodi, his mother's hometown, as a child. As a thank you, Collodi erected the Pinocchio Theme Park to commemorate that association. And that's no lie.

•

Marco, a tall, lanky man with a shaved haircut and the chief waiter at our hotel in Montecatini Terme, stood ready near our table. He possessed a sense of humor as dry as aged Chianti, we would soon learn.

He reminded us of an Italian John Cleese. Furthermore, our cute, young waitress was eager to please, especially in light of our son Jay's presence. Were we living in one of Cleese's classic *Fawlty Towers* sitcom episodes?

Marco's dead-pan humor, or sometimes lack thereof, was mesmerizing to Jackie. She thought the way he delivered his one-line quips about the weather ("Tomorrow: more rain") or the tourist attractions ("My day off I spend at home") were a riot.

After imbibing a glass or two of wine, Jay told him, "Marco, my mother loves you."

Without skipping a beat, while laying down some utensils on our table, Marco replied with a poker face, "I knew this from the first time."

The three of us broke into hysterics while Marco continued nonchalantly serving the other dinner patrons.

Marco's meteorological forecast for Thursday proved to be faulty, though, and that was a bright note to start the day. We finally got to see sunny Italy in a most wondrous way. As the sun rose midmorning over the golden hills of Tuscany on our way to the towers of San Gimignano, its warmth burned off the fog that had crept between the valleys.

When we pulled off the road for a scenic overlook, we were rewarded with a landscape of random cypress trees, sloping vineyards, and ancient olive trees shrouded in a sun-dappled, hazy aura. This lingering memory of the heart of Italy more than offset the muddy splatter on our car afterwards as Jay fishtailed back onto the country lane.

Fully relaxed and now comfortable driving the scenic routes across Tuscany, we felt as if we were the only ones who had chosen this place, this time, this day. We owned *la strada*, the road.

That is, however, until we motored up to San Gimignano and saw the visitors' parking lots practically filled. We then realized that many other tourists had simply arrived earlier and already found their places for the day's activities in the markets and museums.

We hoofed it like billy goats up the hillside until we found an open gate to this unique, walled, medieval version of the Manhattan skyline, the historic center of which is a UNESCO World Heritage site. During its heyday, San Gimignano enjoyed several successes in commercial enterprises as well on the battlefield. Numerous leading families proceeded to construct large towers (as many as seventy-six once overlooked the landscape here) both as a sign of wealth and for defensive purposes. It seemed that not only did the citizens have to ward off invaders, but a few internecine battles were also waged on occasion. Today, fourteen towers still remain standing, helping to maintain the effect of its famous cityscape nearly as it was in the age of the Renaissance.

First, we discovered a hidden gem of a church that is often overlooked in favor of the more famous ones in San Gimignano.

The Church of St. Augustine, built between 1280 and 1298, contains wonderful frescoes depicting the life of this saint. A beautiful marble altar with bas-relief carvings illustrate the miracles of St. Bartholomew. It was sculpted by Benedetto da Maiano, whose name happens to be spelled very similarly to Jackie's maiden name, Miano. We were glad we made this church a stop as part of our San Gimignano tour because of this little vignette associated with her lineage.

Next we caught up with the rest of the crowd in the outdoor market set up in the main piazza. Even though it was not high travel season, the tents and stalls were filled with bargain-hunters, and we were even pleasantly surprised to be able spot in the mix of hundreds of people four of our fellow, intrepid travelers staying at our hotel. They were wheeling and dealing for some shoes when we surprised them.

We then meandered through various vendors' booths at the market, but came up empty handed so we headed to the cultural side of the piazza where a special edifice awaited us: the Collegiata. Formerly a duomo when San Gimignano had an assigned bishop, the Collegiate Church of Santa Maria Assunta is a specially-designated church with origins dating back to the tenth century.

This rather plain-looking (on its exterior) Romanesque house of worship became one of Italy's most-frescoed churches, thanks to several renowned artists together with complementary help from sculptors Benedetto da Maiano and his brother Giuliano. Not only do the frescoes portray twenty-six episodes of the Old Testament as well as a realistic depiction of *The Last Judgment* by Taddeo di Bartolo, but on a wall near the entrance rests a notable one by Domenico Ghirlandaio featuring a local scene that captures many of the original towers of the city as they stood in the fifteenth century.

The supporting arcades and columns within the aisles are a striking composition of alternating stripes of black and white marble. But perhaps the most memorable feature of this former *duomo* is the vaulted ceiling, painted magnificently in deep blue with gold stars twinkling throughout this celestial scene. I half-expected a chorus of angels to descend from these heavens and begin singing sacred hymns.

While no seraphs appeared, a few minutes later as we explored the streets of San Gimignano, its towers looming over us, I happened to look skyward and spotted a real live cherub in an upper window being held by his *nonna*, grandmother. I motioned with my camera and the kindly woman willingly held the baby higher for a photo she would never see, but of which she would probably be immensely proud if she did.

After discovering many of these attractions, galleries, and shops we had worked up an appetite. What better fare in Tuscany for lunch than a bowl of ribollita? We hadn't had any since Monday, three whole days earlier!

Our bellies full, we strolled along a dirt path sandwiched between the city's walls and some olive trees growing on the side of a sloping hill. Jackie decided an olive branch would make a nice souvenir, but in trying to break one off, slipped and nearly fell off the pathway into a mess of olive pits. Luckily, Jay and I managed to catch her as it would have been a very nasty spill down an embankment of thirty feet or more truly the pits.

Pit Tip: "Pahk yah cah in Luccah" as well as in other hill towns like San Gimignano. Even if the euro is strong, it is still a bargain to leave the confines of your auto and see these cities on foot, provided the weather cooperates.

Otherwise, you will spend all your time driving in reverse or squeezing through the narrowest of streets or running into a series of cul-de-sacs.

CHAPTER SIXTEEN

Horse(power) of a Different Color

(Siena, Tuscany)

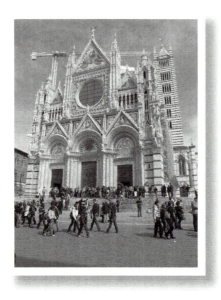

We next drove southeasterly toward Siena, the names of Tuscan towns and villages becoming more and more musical along the way: Pianella, Monteriggioni, and our favorite to pronounce, Poggibonsi.

Once we passed through the main gate of Siena we studied our maps and guidebooks and discovered this was a place where beauty was not only on high but also at our feet. We entered from one of the eleven streets that emptied into the center of town, and, slightly descending below us, we saw the piazza's bricks laid out in nine different patterns symbolizing the Council of Nine, Siena's medieval governing body.

Piazza del Campo is at the heart of Siena, a magnet for tourists. Three-hundred-and-sixty-three days a year, the piazza operates like many others throughout Italy. The other two days, July 2 and August 16, though, the Sienese consider this square to be the center of the universe   the illustrious *Palio di Siena* horse race circles the unique, fan-shaped town center.

Seventeen *contrade* (neighborhoods) compete for first place, pride, and a *palio*, a special, highly coveted silk banner in a locale famous for its flag-throwing pageantry. Actually only ten riders and horses, chosen by lot, run in the first heat of this fierce competition in July, called the *Palio di Provenzano*. The jockeys are clad in bright colors representative of their respective parishes and animals or symbols.

The bypassed contrade can participate in the second event, the *Palio dell'Assunta*, the following month. Prior to the run, all of the horses are blessed inside their respective churches, and a thick layer of dirt is laid in the piazza as a racetrack. Incidentally, it is not a mark of shame to finish last in these two races, but much worse rather to finish second, that is, so close but so far away.

On race day, this signature piazza is jammed with over 25,000 spectators around whom the racers run hell-bent; many jockeys are even thrown from their rides leaving the horses to finish the turns on their own. The event takes only around ninety seconds for three laps around the square, but the pride is forever. Fortunately, the short-lived palio itself is preceded by special foods, knights in armor, and various festivities. Of course, afterward the winners can celebrate as long as they wish and hang their respective banners proudly.

Now that's a horse(power) of a different color.

Looking up within the confines of the Piazza del Campo, we were awestruck by Siena's trademark Palazzo Pubblico and its bell tower, which at nearly 300 feet tall is the second highest in Italy. This town hall is now a museum containing one of the most famous series of fourteenth-century frescoes in the country, *The Allegory of Good and Bad Government* by Ambrogio Lorenzetti. The scenes in these paired paintings show the dichotomy between a utopian, well-managed state and the ruins of a poorly governed one.

The bell tower is called the Torre del Mangia but has nothing to do with food as you might have imagined if you know that *"mangiare"* means "to eat" in Italian. Built to the exact height of the cathedral in Siena to show that the state and church held equal power, the tower is named after its first bell ringer, a rather idle sort of man, whose nickname was *"Mangiaguadagni"* which translates to "profit-eater." Eventually, the name stuck in the shorter version.

The tintinnabulation of the tower's bells reminded us of sounds as from a church, and so it was time for us to make our way a few blocks down a captivating street from the heart of town to the soul of Siena—the Duomo.

Despite the temporary scaffolding and cranes in place, this glorious church was debatably more dazzling than the other classical Gothic one we had seen previously in Orvieto. Or was it that day's sun? Or was it the sun symbol centered between the archway of the main entrance and the rose window above? This sun represents the risen Christ; St. Bernardino of Siena wanted it to be used as a unifying force among the ever-feuding contrade.

We see several resemblances between the facades of each duomo, such as three portals with recessed archways, dozens of carved statues, four steeples, a rose window, and alternating black-and-white patterns.

However, a few distinctions remain. For instance, Siena's cathedral has the unusual pink marble from the local area adorning its walls. Also the pulpit in Siena's sanctuary is a phenomenal series of carvings depicting the life of Christ done by Nicola Pisano in the mid-thirteenth century and is considered to be the masterpiece of this leader in the Italian Renaissance revival. Ornate altars, too many to count, marble pillars, and stained glass windows provide the eye with overstimulation impossible to absorb in an afternoon—visitors must take a course to learn everything about this cathedral.

However, what really floored us was underfoot, and it was not in the basement. Inlaid marble mosaics of biblical scenes divided into fifty-six panels cover the entire footprint of the Duomo. Forty artists with intense religious dedication completed the opus over a period of two-hundred years. We were blessed to be able to view it during tourist off-season since the masterpieces are fully revealed only when foot traffic is lighter.

While in town, we purchased a watercolor of the Siena Duomo to add to our collection of Italian churches. It was a simple human rendering of only the exterior of what had to be a divinely-inspired work of art by these masters.

Pit Tip: Driving through the Tuscan countryside offers an unforgettable pleasure, witnessing the incomparable landscape and the wonders of these hill towns. If you have a chance to visit, do yourself a favor and rent a car so you can wander between the villages and linger in each for as long as you wish.

Pit Tip: Simply put: don't drink and drive in Italy. Appoint a *l'autista designato* (designated driver), or walk, take a train, bus or taxi if you've been drinking. Otherwise, even one glass of wine or *limoncello* can cause a person to reach the minimum blood alcohol content (BAC) of .05 milligrams, enough to be heavily fined hundreds in euros.

CHAPTER SEVENTEEN

Checking the Brakes

(Le Cinque Terre)

The source of the Carrara marble used in the classic statues and edifices by Michelangelo and other sculptors of the Renaissance was visible to us in the mountains to our right as we exited Pisa and headed north along the Ligurian coast toward Le Cinque Terre. The white striations of the peaks appeared as snow from a distance. It boggled our minds how hundreds of years ago they were able to mine the marble and then transport it over such long distances, considering its extensive weight.

Within an hour or so, we arrived in La Spezia, an industrialized city with an important harbor for commerce and the Italian navy. The leitmotif throughout our travels has been to climb every mountain and ford every stream to follow our dream destinations. That day was no exception as we braved hairpin turns above the port of La Spezia up to a heavily forested mountaintop. On an adjacent peak, what appeared to be an inaccessible castle stood out among the fall foliage. I kept praying the car rental people had checked the tires and brakes before they released our car, and then calmed myself by realizing that our rented Fiat was a relatively brand new vehicle.

After about twenty minutes of harrowing turns, curves, and switchbacks, we spotted signs for Riomaggiore, the first of the "five lands." *Le Cinque Terre* represents five out-of-the-way villages, a romantic venue for relaxing (*after* the drive up the mountains). We shifted into lower gear as we steered downward into the city limits and found the public parking garage.

Perhaps it was because we were sort of living in our own little operatic world, but we always managed to find some type of conflict. This time we irritated the gatekeeper of the parking lot when we snuck behind another car while the gate was still raised. That was two cars too quickly for the attendant, so we pleaded ignorance and begged forgiveness. Fortunately we succeeded in finding one of the last spaces of the day in the garage.

The walk into this village was non-eventful, and that was the whole idea. This chain of remote towns appears as they were a hundred years ago: no fast food joints, a few tourist shops but nothing garish or overwhelming. It took us about ten minutes to stroll downhill and then even farther down toward the train station.

This leg of the trip between Riomaggiore and Manarola, incidentally, is the best one for hiking versus taking the train. It is a breathtaking mile-and-a-half trail called the *Via dell'Amore (Pathway of Love)*, high above the sea, carved into, above, and sometimes under rock overhangs. On this *bella giornata* (beautiful day) the temperature rose to bathing suit weather as we noticed sun worshippers hundreds of feet below us on a flat rock close to the Ligurian shore.

The aquamarine sea and deep blue sky that composers always write about was all ours to absorb. The scenery appeared as romantic as the name implies, and I added Jackie's initials and mine with the scratch of a hotel ballpoint pen into the rocks where other lovers have painted or etched theirs. If I could have chosen music for this setting, it likely would have been arias from my favorite Puccini opera, *La Boheme.*

We caught the train and decided to go to the last fishing village, Monterosso al Mare. Later we planned to work our way back to the remaining two hamlets aboard the local railway.

Monterosso al Mare is a little more upscale than its sister villages, and the closest of the *Cinque Terre* towns in relation to the jet-set capital of the Italian Riviera, Portofino. The beachfront is accented by dark sand and outcroppings in the nearby water and is populated by a combination of strolling tourists and motionless sunbathers. The boardwalk bustled with tour groups frequenting the shops and restaurants. It reminded us of the more commercialized Amalfi Coast towns such as Positano and Ravello.

We paused to take pictures of each other without our jackets and sweaters so we could prove how warm the weather was for the folks back home; then we bought Italian ice cream cones to add to the atmosphere. The unanimous choice: a vanilla-flavored *gelato* laced with chocolate shavings called *stracciatella. Delizioso!*

We walked with our cones into the main square and did some window shopping and neck-craning at the old stucco buildings that overlook welcoming squares. How can some structure hundreds of years old still look so inviting, despite laundry hanging out the window? The street scene was so typically Italian.

Next stop: Vernazza.

Aah . . . Vernazza. Not too ritzy but not so run-of-the-mill either—just right for relaxing. Jackie and Jay could hardly believe that the maestro of this family saga, who had directed them this wonderful week around half of Italy, wanted to introduce the word "relax" into his opus.

We all agreed that Vernazza got the nod for the most "*aahs*" and was our favorite of the four unique Cinque Terre communities we had managed to see on this trip.

In each direction there were serene scenes. To our backs and overlooking *the center*, striated rock formations gave way to patches of green vegetation here and there and then to brown earth upon which grapevines grew.

A small fishing boat painted a dark blue with a striking turquoise on the interior rested in the still water at harbor-side, its outboard motor silent. The waterfront serves as the main plaza and everything revolves around it, including the sidewalks. People stooped under a low natural bridge with a cave-like entrance to the beach from the main street.

Others like us were content to walk to the edge of harbor and sit on the huge jetty that protects the area. A simple, tall church with a miniature dome rose on our left as we looked back toward the town, blending in with the soft pink and ochre stucco apartments and storefronts. Large, colorful umbrellas shaded diners at sea level. Adventurous sightseers took the challenge to climb a thirty-foot rock formation to reach a restaurant built atop, and then dined there with a bird's-eye view of the sea.

The winds were calm that day, so a handful of anchored pleasure boats merely bobbed in the placid water and added to the serenity. In the distance a few miles away, a plume of smoke from an unknown source in the high-pitched mountaintops hovered over Monterosso al Mare snuggled below. Even the approach of a tour boat entering the port at Vernazza did not detract from this tranquil scene but instead told us we were simply part of the view of the beautiful setting of Vernazza as seen by those aboard the vessel.

However, our reverie had to come to an end. On the way to the train station, we stopped in a coffee bar to buy a couple bottles of water, and we noticed a most unusual photograph of Vernazza decorating the wall: one that depicted snow covering the entire landscape. The proprietor said that this event took place some twenty to thirty years ago, but it was hard to imagine given the day we were experiencing.

We took a little bit of *Le Cinque Terre* back with us as a keepsake to enjoy at a later meal in our home: a small bag of dried herbs with which to make a delicious pesto sauce for which this area is well-known.

Pit Tip: Hurry to **Le Cinque Terre** then slow down once you get there. Fortunately, despite the influx of more tourists in recent years who discovered this UNESCO World Heritage site, the hideaway has not become as commercialized as Portofino, the jet-set capital of the Italian Riviera, farther up the coast.

It's a special place, a romantic place for relaxing (after the drive up from La Spezia), and the slow movement of *la dolce vita* **(the sweet life)**.

And don't forget to ask the car rental people to **double-check** the tires and brakes before they release the car to you. The windy roads of the Cinque Terre are not where you want to find out your brakes aren't working.

Pit Tip: Best methods for parking a car on a hill in addition to pulling up the emergency brake. Since most people do so on the right hand side of the street, shift your manual transmission stick into first gear in order to park uphill and turn the front wheels toward the sidewalk curb so that they point left.

If the vehicle is pointed downhill, put the car into reverse to park and turn the front wheels so that they point right. In either scenario, should your car roll, it will roll into the sidewalk curb.

CHAPTER EIGHTEEN

Buying Self-Serve Fuel on Sundays & Returning the Rental Car

(Bologna)

Toward the end of the trip, we found ourselves just a few kilometers from our planned departure from the Bologna airport and we needed to fill our rental car tank with *benzina* (gas).

Jay spotted a gas station, but the sign, unfortunately, read *"chiuso"* (closed) instead of *"aperto"* (open), not surprising since it was a Sunday and gas stations are invariably closed in Italy on Sundays. Another nearby placard, however, indicated that it was a 24-hour, self-service facility, so we pulled into the driveway ready to pump some gas.

What followed next would end up being so hilarious and dumbfounding that Jackie, with her own self-serving agenda, decided to capture the moment on camera, unbeknownst to Jay and me. The eventual pictures indicated two of us wearing theatrical masks of perplexity trying to figure out how to initiate the pumping process and then pay at these unattended gas tanks.

First, we scratched our heads when the screen asked for a pin number (which we did not have) for our credit (not debit) card.

Several minutes into our gas station adventure, a middle-aged Italian gentleman drove up to the pumps just as we decided to deposit our last wad of euros in a vain attempt to fill up the tank completely. We had somehow hit the button for that gentleman's gas pump.

Eventually through sign language and Jay's Italian vocabulary, we managed to set the record straight as to who had paid what amount and how many liters we got for our respective cars.

Even today, I still try to avoid having to fill up the tank to return the rental car on a Sunday if possible—who needs that kind of stress on the last day of vacation?

•

As we returned to the Bologna airport, unfortunately, our tank was not quite full; our cash supply had allowed us to fill it up only to the three-quarter mark. After leaving the car in the rental garage, we headed inside to pay the bill. We were shocked to learn about a thirty euro charge for gas from the agency to fill the tank, plus another ten euros just for completing the paperwork. Use of a credit card with a poor exchange rate only compounded the problem.

Jay suddenly turned on the charm and began speaking Italian to try to cajole the dark-eyed female clerk into relenting, politely saying that the charges were absurd. He finally convinced her with a smile and she waived the extra fee. Still, it cost us over forty dollars just to fill a quarter of a tank.

The young woman conceded that we could go back into the city and fill it up ourselves, but Jay told her that we didn't have enough euros left to meet the minimum ten-euro charge on the pumps. In fact, we had precisely nine euros and twenty cents to be exact, all in loose change, which wouldn't even operate the gas pumps.

She took the coins from Jay and handed him a ten-euro note with a winsome smile. The result: a happy ending to the plot as Jay proceeded to get the car, return to the station and, for that amount (about fifteen dollars), was able to top off the tank.

Pit Tip: Remember that gas stations are *chiuso* **(closed)** on Sunday, so drivers are on their own. Always have plenty of cash when pulling into a gas station on that day of the week in case the credit/debit card machines aren't working or you can't manage to work them.

Most importantly, be sure to pump the right fuel for your vehicle: using diesel for a car with a regular engine, or vice versa, can ruin your day, not to mention the car. Look for *senza piombo* (unleaded) or *verde* (green). For a diesel-powered car, ask for *diesel* or *gasolio*.

Finally, consider having someone with you to take some candid camera shots of your gas pumping attempts, just in case you, too, end up with a funny story out of it. Otherwise, people may think you're full of bologna.

Pit Tip: If you happen to have a handsome son who speaks a little *italiano*, be sure to bring him with you to Italy to help negotiate. You never know when a little sweet talk in the vernacular will go a long way with a female clerk.

If not, the advice remains to be sure to have enough euros to top off your rental car's gas tank before handing it in; otherwise the additional fees are outrageous and you may not find as forgiving a clerk as we did.

Hotel Guide

ABRUZZO

Best Western Hotel Plaza (★★★★); Piazza Sacro Cuore, 55; Pescara; http://www.plazapescara.it. Conveniently located to both the airport and train station, the Hotel Plaza in Pescara offers great value accommodations. Guests may easily walk to the Adriatic as well as to several retail and restaurant destinations. The city of Pescara is part modern seacoast resort complete with Prada-class boutiques, part university town, and part successful, industrialized area. The sixty-eight-room Hotel Plaza offers various room types including Classic, Comfort, Junior Suite, and Business. Amenities include air conditioning, bicycles for hire, free Hospitality Bar, free Wi-Fi internet connection and limited free parking, as well as no-smoking room options, all comfortable, stylish and quiet, meeting Best Western standards. The Plaza specializes in meetings, conferences and, perhaps, most importantly, family reunions.

AMALFI COAST / CAMPANIA

Casa Raffaele Conforti (★★★★); Via Casa Mannini, 10; Maiori (SA); http://www.casaraffaeleconforti.it. Casa Raffaele Conforti was built in the 19th century as a villa for a rich lemon merchant. The room décor features antique furnishings of the original Conforti family as well as modern style options. Several of the bedchambers have fifteen-foot high ceilings and walls lavishly decorated with Baroque-era frescoes. Double doors, nearly as high and festooned with wind-blown sheers, open to wrought iron balconies adorned with seasonal flowerpots, a perfect place to relax over a glass of wine. Antique Venetian glass chandeliers act as prisms, catching the fading rays of the day's sun, and provide lighting for these romantic rooms. Such lavish quarters give you a sense of royalty amid the town of Maiori, a lesser-known gem along the Amalfi Coast. Moreover, Casa Raffaele Conforti has its own private beach equipped with sunbeds and umbrellas and is convenient to nearby shops and tourist attractions.

CALABRIA

Hotel Miramare (★★★★); Via C. Colombo, 2/A; Marina di Gioiosa Ionica (RC); http://www.miramarehotel.biz. Located across the street from the Ionian Sea, the Hotel Miramare has undergone recent renovations, including an open staircase centered in a three-story atrium. Through open windows, sea breezes carry in the soothing sounds of waves lapping the shore like a lullaby that helps you fall into a deep sleep at night. The hotel offers thirty-six rooms with private terraces, of which nine are suites. Amenities include air-conditioning, satellite TV, telephone, internet, strongbox, mini-bar, and an exclusive beach area for guests.

LAZIO

Hotel Quirinale (★★★★); Via Nazionale, 7; Rome; http://www. hotelquirinale.it. Located on a main thoroughfare in the center of Rome, the Quirinale Hotel is convenient to the Termini train station and nearby attractions, sports options, and theaters. Built in 1865, the Quirinale has a rich history and its guests over time have included famous opera stars—the hotel has a rear passage to the adjacent Opera House. The hotel's grandeur is reflected in its 209 elegant rooms and suites, haute cuisine, wrought iron bannisters, Persian rugs, and exotic gardens. Amenities include concierge service, complimentary breakfast, fitness center, business and meeting facilities, laundry, and safe deposit box.

Mecenate Palace Hotel (★★★★); Via Carlo Alberto, 3; Rome; http:// www.mecenatepalace.com. Enjoy a complimentary buffet breakfast or savor other dining and cocktails from the Mecenate Palace Hotel Roof Garden, which offers a spectacular view of nearby Piazza Santa Maria Maggiore and a 360-degree panorama of Rome. The hotel is conveniently located a walkable distance from the Rome train station as well as to many famous sites of the Eternal City and features seventy-four guest rooms in a variety of options from Single Classic to Executive or Luxury level, plus suites and apartments. Amenities include air conditioning, satellite TV, Wi-Fi, telephone and radio, safe, and hairdryer.

UMBRIA

Le Tre Vaselle Resort & SPA (★★★★★); Via Garibaldi, 48; Torgiano (PG); http://www.3vaselle.it. If Italy is famous for its food and wine, Le Tre Vaselle Resort & SPA represents the epitome of Italian cuisine and vineyards. The Lungarotti family is internationally acclaimed for its Umbrian wines and olive oils, defining farm-to-table dining and hospitality. Located in a carefully-restored, 17th-century brick building in the heart of Torgiano, Le Tre Vaselle exudes charm and character and features agrotourism, museums, and a wine bar and shop. The ambience of the rooms reminds travelers of aristocratic country houses of yesterday.

SICILY

Hotel Villa Athena (★★★★★); Via Passeggiata Archeologica, 33; Agrigento; http://www.hotelvillaathena.it. The five-star Hotel Villa Athena sits less than a mile from the Temple of Concordia, the closest of any of the ruins and one of the best-preserved Greek temples in all of Europe. I highly recommend asking for room # 205, whose terrace offers the most priceless view of the spectacular, spot-lit temple in all its glory. The hotel was originally an 18th century villa set among fields of arugula and olive groves near the site of an ancient Greek cistern. A variety of spa services provide a combination of treatments for both the aesthetics and well-being of the face and body.

Hotel Villa Diodoro (★★★★); Via Bagnoli Croci, 75; Taormina (ME); http://www.hotelvilladiodoro.com. The Hotel Villa Diodoro may be a little difficult to find amid the tight streets of Taormina, but it's well worth it. Ask for a room with a balcony, which overlooks the pool and affords a spectacular vista of the Ionian Sea and Mt. Etna, topped off with clouds, hazy in the distance. It's only a few minutes walk to the ancient Greco-Roman amphitheater, the historical center of town, the public gardens, and the main thoroughfare, Corso Umberto. Enjoy the hotel's swimming pool, a private pebbled beach, restaurant, bars, and its Wellness Point—access to a complete spa amenity with two massage rooms and a fully equipped gym with the latest "techno gym" cardio equipment.

Jolly Aretusa Palace Hotel (★★★★); Corso Gelone, 42; Siracusa; http://www.jollyaretusapalacehotel.com. The Jolly Aretusa Palace Hotel touts its brand new spa, a "sanctuary to calm your mind and spirit," featuring a jacuzzi, treatment cabins, sauna, Turkish baths, and more. Conveniently located near the historical Greek ruins of Siracusa, the hotel offers local gastronomic dining pleasures in its "Five Senses" restaurant, including free breakfast. Other amenities include free parking, meeting rooms, satellite television, safety deposit box, laundry, air conditioning, non-smoking rooms, and hair dryer.

Mondello Palace Hotel (★★★★), Viale Principe di Scalea; Palermo; http://www.mondellopalacehotel.it. Long sheer curtains billow through the casement windows in the hotel rooms and hallways as guests stroll through convenient alleyways and benches among the redolent, exotic flowerbeds and gardens, which feature a picturesque fountain with goldfish and water lilies, toward the private beachfront. The Mondello Palace Hotel is also renowned for its restaurant, swimming pool, and free Wi-Fi connection. The bathing resort of Mondello has a golden sandy beach. Sun beds, umbrellas, and water sports are available for guests' convenience.

Acknowledgments

I would like to thank Kari Hock and Michelle Fabio for believing in the concept of the unique genre of *Pit Stops, Pitfalls and Olive Pits* and for their editorial support and advice. I also appreciate the special talent of Sharon Mentyka for her creative cover illustration.

To my son, Jay, and to my dear friends, Joe and Jean St. Clair, many thanks for coming along for the ride, literally. None of these vignettes would have been possible without your presence.

Finally, I cannot express enough my love and appreciation for my beautiful wife, Jackie, who is not only a great editor and fun vacationer, but also my traveling partner as we drive though life together.

Photo Credits

A special thank you to Linda Martinez, Diana Strinati Baur, Faith Griswold, David Hock, and Melissa Muldoon for their photos.

Glossary

abbondanza - abundance

al fresco - outdoors, open air

amari - bitters

amore - love

anno - year

antipasti - appetizers

aperto - open

arrividerci - good-bye

assaggino - sample appetizer

Autogrill - rest stop

autostrada - freeway

bambini - children

barista- coffee shop server

basso profundo - bass opera
    singer

bella - beautiful

benzina - gasoline

bistecca - steak

bottega - shop

braciola - steak, chop

brutta figura - bad impression

buona fortuna - good luck

calciatore - soccer player

caldo - warm

campagna - countryside

canestrini - type of pasta or
    biscuits

cannoli - cream-filled pastry

capisco – I understand

caprese – mozzarella/tomato/
    basil salad

carabiniere - Italian military
    police officer

casa - house, home

cassata – Sicilian cake with
    ricotta, candies, chocolate

cento - hundred

centro - town center

chiuso - closed

ciao - hello, good-bye

cinque - five

cioccolato - chocolate

città - city

collegiata - specially-designated
    church

comune - town, municipality

contrada - neighborhood, quarter
    of town

corso - main street

crostini - toast with spread
    topping

cucina - kitchen

delizioso - delicious

destra - right

dolci - sweets, desserts

dov''e - where is

due - two

duomo - cathedral

espresso - coffee

fagioli – beans

la multa – traffic ticket

farfalla - butterfly (and butterfly-
    shaped pasta)

fiore - flower

fiume - river

gasolio – diesel

gelato - ice cream

giardini - gardens

gnocchi – potato dumplings

grazie – thank you

intermezzo - interval,
    intermission

introduzione - introduction

involtini - roll

limoncello - lemon liqueur

liquirizia - licorice

madre - mother

majolica – type of pottery

mangia – eat!

mia/mio - my

mille - a thousand

nazionale - national

nero - black

nonna - grandmother

numero - number

osteria - tavern

palio - horse race

palazzo – palace, large building

panettone - Christmas cake

panelle - fritter, croquette

paparazzo – celebrity
    photographer

parco - park

parcheggio - car park, parking
    space

passeggiata – walk (noun)

pasta e fagioli - pasta with beans

pasticceria - pastry shop

pazzo - crazy, mad

cent'anni - a hundred years

per favore - please

piazza – town square

prego – you're welcome; "after you"

prima donna - leading operatic lady

preparazione - preparation

profiterole - creampuff

prosecco – dry, sparkling wine

pubblico - public

ragazza - girl

ragazzo - boy

representante - representative, salesperson

ribollita - bean, cabbage, and bread soup

rucola - arugula

scusi - excuse me, pardon me

senza piombo – unleaded (gas)

sì - yes

signore - sir, a man

signora – ma'am, woman

sinistra - left

sfogliatelle - flaky pastry

stracciatella - anilla gelato with chocolate bits

strada - street

tagliatelle - wide noodle, pasta

tarantella - lively folk dance

telefonino - cell (mobile) phone

terre - lands

torre - tower

torrone - honey/almond candy

trattoria - small restaurant

uno - one

uscita - exit

verde – green (unleaded gas)

via - road, street

vino - wine

vita - life

About the Author

John Tabellione is an award-winning, professional freelance writer and blogger with a broad international background.

In addition to his driving experiences throughout Italy (Roma, Firenze, Perugia, Pisa, Le Cinque Terre, Assisi, Cortona, Orvieto, Pescara, Reggio di Calabria, Ravello, Taormina, Siracusa, Palermo, Agrigento), he has also accrued extensive European auto travel in Germany, France, Austria, and Luxembourg. John's other international travels include residency in Germany and Turkey, as well as having traveled to Greece, England, Croatia, Hong Kong, China, Mexico and Canada.

A member of the Atlanta Writers Club and the North Point Writers' Critique Group, he has earned awards for both his nonfiction and fiction writing: Atlanta Writers Club (First Place Award); Georgia Writers Association (Third Place Certificate); Central Atlanta Progress, Inc. Writing Contest (Runner-up Prize).

John's blog, "Tabs on Writing," provides a light-hearted approach to grammar, punctuation, spelling, homophones, and word derivations, weaving grammatical advice through anecdotal news stories from the past and present.

His writing expertise is complemented by over twenty-five years of professional communications responsibilities as a marketing and sales executive with Fortune 500 companies.

John holds a B.A. degree in English from Fairfield University and an MBA in Marketing from the University of Hartford. He has also completed an Italian language and culture program at Kennesaw State University as well as intensive Russian studies at Syracuse University.

He and his wife, Jackie, are parents of two adult sons: Jay, who traveled on one of the journeys to Italy; and Justin, married to Courtney, who are parents to Allison Sophia and Taylor Lucia.